Harry Price in the uniform of an Able Seaman at the turn of the century

THE
ROYAL TOUR
— 1901 —

OR THE CRUISE OF
H.M.S. OPHIR

BEING A LOWER DECK ACCOUNT OF THEIR
ROYAL HIGHNESSES, THE DUKE AND DUCHESS OF CORNWALL AND YORK'S
VOYAGE AROUND THE BRITISH EMPIRE

C. 1

Petty Officer HARRY PRICE

WILLIAM MORROW AND COMPANY, INC.
New York

© 1980 Jack Price

First published in Great Britain 1980 by Webb & Bower
(Publishers) Limited, Exeter, England

Library of Congress Catalog Card Number 79-49267
ISBN 0-688-03667-8

Printed and bound in Italy by Arnoldo Mondadori Editore

Harry Price 1877–1965

Harry Price was born in Birmingham in 1877. His parents came from Welsh families who had emigrated from their country to the expanding industrial city of Birmingham, where his father became a master builder. The family produced several "romantics", at least one of whom became a minor poet and another, Harry's brother, a Royal Academician. Many were skilled anglers and having settled in Birmingham were obliged to change from game to coarse fishing. In the latter field they eventually became the "champion fishing family of Birmingham".

Harry's artistic ability was noted by his schoolmaster and he was sent to the Birmingham School of Art, where in a couple of weeks he progressed right through the School, from bottom to top class. He was then told that he had such natural talent that they couldn't teach him anything. This only added to his growing dislike of Birmingham, "the land of bricks and mortar," so he left home in 1893 and joined the Royal Navy as a Boy. Except to attend his mother's funeral he never returned.

Stationed at Devonport he found the fulfilment of his subconscious longings on his door-step in the countryside of Devon and Cornwall. On his leaves and any free time he walked for miles along the Cornish coastal footpaths and over Dartmoor, and in later life often remembered that the sight of a young sailor walking for pleasure before the turn of the century aroused much interest.

Dartmoor was the main attraction, and one of his favourite excursions was diagonally across the moor from Plymouth to the Chagford area. He always travelled light, with little or no money but with a little fishing tackle and painting materials. Thus he could always catch food – he was an expert at cooking fish on the river bank – and earn his keep by painting. Eventually he found Fingle Gorge (he never travelled with a map) and the account of his discovery of Fingle Bridge and Drewsteignton is most moving. He wept on arrival at the bridge over the River Teign and the Church bells seemed to welcome him at Drewsteignton where he went to morning service, and he silently vowed that this was where he would make his home when he left the Navy. Those same bells were to ring specially for him over twenty years later when he made a triumphant return to his "home" village after distinguished service in the Great War. Although he travelled virtually all over the world in the course of his service life, he remained true to this vow and still declared that nowhere in the world was more attractive to him.

Although he was a loyal and true patriot he joined the Navy "to see the world" rather than to serve his country and he often rebelled against naval discipline, as his service record shows. He once led a minor mutiny but was pardoned because he was also responsible for ending it, when it began to reach ugly proportions.

In 1899 he joined the *Britannia*, the senior of two training ships moored in the river Dart, which were the forerunners of the present Royal Naval College at Dartmouth. On this ship his good record and rapid promotion probably led to his being chosen as a member of the crew of the *Ophir* for the Royal Tour of 1901. He served on that ship from February to November 1901. On leaving the Royal Navy in 1907 he joined the Royal Fleet Reserve and was called up for service in the Great War on 2nd August, 1914.

During that war he served in five ships, three of which were sunk within the space of nine months. These included the *Ocean* and the *Majestic* and from the former he was picked up by destroyer after fourteen hours in the water. He was a superb natural swimmer and, being born with a caul, always declared: "I could never drown." He was demobilized in March 1919 after he had been awarded the Distinguished Service Medal for his services.

For an ordinary seaman he made his service career a very colourful one, for besides the Royal Tour he travelled extensively and grasped every opportunity to see the world. He even lived for a short while with cowboys in Texas after he had passed their test of outdrinking them in a saloon bar in Houston, and he spent a short time in an Indian Reserve in North America where he painted designs and emblems on wigwams.

After settling in Drewsteignton he declared: "I had no wish to wander any more – only up and down the banks of the river Teign, fishing for salmon and trout." He was a talented naturalist and made a fine collection of butterflies and birds' eggs. Because of this and his ability to climb well he worked for a while as a free-lance egg collector for Watkins and Doncaster of the Strand, London. This led, in turn, to an association with Richard Kearton, the pioneer bird photographer, and thus he experienced the transition from egg collecting to bird photography.

On the river Teign he quickly adapted his coarse fishing knowledge to game fishing – the reverse of his Birmingham forbears – and in a few years became the finest angler on the river (his fishing diaries, covering about forty years, make very interesting and informative reading). He was still able to practise coarse fishing, however, at a famous local carp pool and one of the best known books on carp fishing is largely about his escapades there, although the identity of the man and the pool are disguised. He also became an expert gardener and his produce sometimes went to the Royal Horticultural Society's shows in London, as non-competitive exhibits. In his later years he grew all his own tobacco – he was a moderately heavy pipe smoker – and cured it by a method based on his knowledge of what he had seen in the tobacco industries of Havana and Rhodesia.

All the while he painted, mainly in oils, and made a number of interesting models, when he had time and "when the spirit moves me". Perhaps his greatest work is a model of his first ship, HMS *Impregnable*, a fully rigged three-decker, which off and on took about seven years to complete. His most ingenious model was of the ship in which he used to smuggle tobacco out of the dockyard. In addition he took up wood carving when he was well over seventy years of age and after a five-year disability, following a stroke at the age of eighty-three, he was still making simple sketches as he lay in his hospital bed up to the time that he died in June 1965, at the age of eighty-eight.

JACK PRICE
Fingle Bridge, Devon

Name *Harry Price* Conduct.

Mog. NP/SC. 23638.
S.—459 (late S.—536). (Revised—March, 1918).
True copy from Admiralty Records.
· · · · CERTIFICATE of the Service of · ·
Harry Price in the Royal Navy.

The corner of this Certificate is to be cut off if the man is discharged with a "Bad" character or with disgrace, or if specially directed by the Admiralty. If the corner is cut off, the fact is to be noted in the Ledger.

Port Division *Devonport.* Official Number 174,854.

Date of Birth 6 February 1877
Where born — Parish *Birmingham* Town or County *Warwick*
Usual place of Residence
Trade brought up to *Painter & Decorator*
Religious Denomination
Can Swim
Man's signature on discharge to pension

Character and Ability on 31st December yearly, on final discharge, and other occasions prescribed by regulation. If recommended for Medal and Gratuity, "R.M.G." to be awarded on 31st December and final discharge, and a line to be drawn across column.

Second Class for Conduct inclusive dates		Ability in Rating, noting substantive rating in brackets			
From	To	Character		Whether R.M.G. or not	Date	Captain's Signature
		V.g			8 Dec 94	
		V.g			5 Feb 95	
		V.g			31 Dec 95	
		Good			31 Dec 96	
		V.g			31 Dec 97	
		V.g			8 Dec 98	
		V.g			8 Dec 99	
		V.g			31 Dec 00	
		V.g			31 Dec 01	
		V.g			31 Dec 02	
		V.g			31 Dec 03	

Good Conduct Badges						
Date	1st, 2nd, 3rd	Granted, Deprived, Restored	Character			Date
			Good			31 Dec 04
			V.g			31 Dec 05
			V.g			31 Dec 06
1 Jan 99	1st	Granted	V.g			8 Feb 07
12 Feb 03	2nd	Granted	V.g	Sat		31 Dec 14
27 Feb 04	2nd	Deprived	Good	Supr		31 Dec 15
28 Apl 04	1st	Deprived	V.g	Sat		31 Dec 16
20 Apl 05	1st	Restored	V.g	Supr		31 Dec 17
19 Oct 05	2nd	Restored	V.g	Supr		31 Dec 18
9 Feb 15	2nd	Deprived	V.g			28 Feb 19
10 Aug 15	2nd	Restored				
10 Aug 17	3rd	Granted				

Continuous Service and Special Service Engagements

Date of actually volunteering	Commencement of time	Period volunteered for	Date received or forfeited	Nature of Decoration
27 July 1893	6 Feb 95	12 years	March 24th 1919	Distinguished Service Medal
			12 APR 1922	1914-15 Star British War Medal Victory Medal

	Date	P.P.P.	Days	Date	P.P.P.	Days	Date	P.P.P.	Days	Date	P.P.P.	Days
Time	9 Oct 96	C	6									
Forfeited												

Description of Person

	Stature Feet In.	Chest In.	Colour of			Marks, Wounds, and Scars
			Hair	Eyes	Complexion	
On Entry as a Boy	5 4½		Lt Brn	Blue	Fresh	Clasped hands, heart & anchor on Lt forearm
On advancement to man's rating, or on entry under 28 years	5 7		Brown			
On re-entry for C.S. or for Non-C.S. after attaining 28 years						
Further description if necessary						

N. 42718/15.
Sta. 303/16.
Sta. 23/18.

Name *Harry Price*

Ship's Name	List and No.		Rating	From	To	Cause of Discharge
Impregnable	15	6163	Boy II	27 July 93	5 Sep 94	
			Boy I	6 Sep 94	3 Dec 94	
Colossus	16	317	"	4 Dec 94	13 Dec 94	
Vivid	15'	3518	"	14 Dec 94	17 Dec 94	
Trafalgar	5	424	"	18 Dec 94	5 Feb 95	
			Ord. Smn	6 Feb 95	28 Mch 96	
Cruiser	16	877	"	24 Mch 96	31 Aug 96	
Trafalgar	5	155	A B	1 Sep 96	11 Sep 97	
Royal Sovereign	5	133	"	12 Sep 97	3 Feb 98	
Vivid I	15	1425	"	4 Feb 98	19 Apl 98	
Cambridge	15	5665	"	20 Apl 98	22 Oct 98	
Defiance	14	2112	"	23 Oct 98	25 Feb 99	
Vivid I	15	5423	"	26 Feb 99	1 May 99	
Britannia	5	93	"	2 May 99	25 May 00	
	"	"	Ldg. Smn	26 May 00	28 Jan 01	
	"	"	P.O. II	29 Jan 01	21 Feb 01	
Vivid I	15	4135	"	22 Feb 01	25 Feb 01	
Ophir	5	97	"	26 Feb 01	6 Nov 01	
Vivid	15'	4982	"	7 Nov 01	1 Feb 02	
Cambridge	15	4135	"	2 Feb 02	3 Feb 02	
Defiance	14	3584	"	4 Feb 02	5 Apl 02	
Vivid	15'	630	"	6 Apl 02	4 June 02	
Ariadne	5	16	"	5 June 02	30 June 03	
Warrior	12ª	2	"	1 July 03	11 Aug 03	
Vivid I	15'	2450	"	12 Aug 03	4 Nov 03	
Donegal	5	68	"	5 Nov 03	5 Feb 04	
	"	"	Ldg. Smn	6 Feb 04	19 Apl 04	
Donegal	5	68	A B	20 Apl 04	6 Jan 05	
Vivid I	15²	14948	"	7 Jan 05	12 Feb 05	
Defiance	14	6356	"	13 Feb 05	20 May 05	
Vivid	15²	1770	"	21 May 05	10 July 05	
New Zealand	5	256	"	11 July 05	12 Jan 07	
Vivid I	15²	5692	"	13 Jan 07	8 Feb 07	Shore C.S. expired
Joined R.F.R. Devonport 15/754 9 February 1907						
Re-enrolled 9 February 12 to serve to 8 February 1917 (S.T.)						
Ocean		101	A B	2 Aug 14	18 Mch 15	
Majestic	14	206	"	19 Mch 15	27 May 15	
Vivid I	15	531	"	28 May 15	9 July 15	
Defiance	14	202	"	10 July 15	13 Sep 15	
Liverpool	5²	2	"	14 Sep 15	28 Mch 19	demobilised

Date	Wounds received in Action and Hurt Certificate; also any meritorious Service, Special recommendation, Prize or other Grants	Captain's Signature
3-11-20	Paid £12-10 s. — d. Naval Prize Fund.	
14 OCT 1922	Final Share of Naval Prize Fund Paid.	
26 OCT 1928	Supplementary Prize Share Paid.	

Awarded R.F.R. Gratuity of £50 Mar 18
Awarded R.F.R. 2nd Grat of £50 Oct 20

Date	Particulars	Captain's Signature	Date	Particulars	Captain's Signature

The certificate of the service of Harry Price in the Royal Navy 1893-1919

"THE ROYAL TOUR"

HONI · SOIT · QUI · MAL · Y · PENSE

OR THE CRUISE
OF
"H.M.S. OPHIR"

BEING A LOWER DECK ACCOUNT, OF THEIR ROYAL HIGHNESSES, THE DUKE AND DUCHESS OF CORNWALL AND YORK'S, VOYAGE AROUND THE BRITISH EMPIRE.
1901

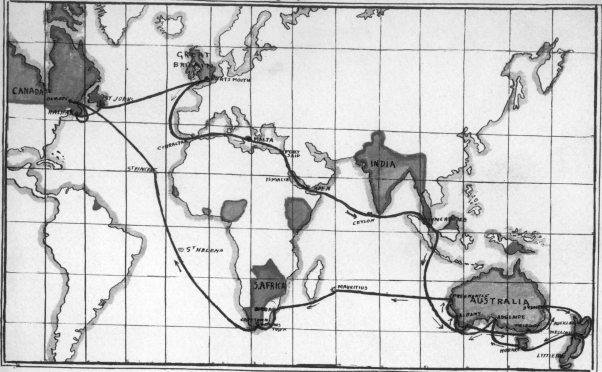

Chart showing line of route, distance covered about 40000 Mls.

NAME OF PLACE	DATE OF ARRIVAL	DATE OF DEPARTURE	NAME OF PLACE	DATE OF ARRIVAL	DATE OF DEPARTURE
Portsmouth		16th Mch	Auckland	11th June	16th June
Gibraltar	20th Mch	22nd Mch	Wellington	17th "	21st "
Malta	25th Mch	27th Mch	Lyttleton	22nd "	24th "
Port Said	30th Mch	31st Mch	Hobart	2nd July	6th July
Suez	1st Apr	1st Apr	Adelaide	8th "	15th "
Aden	5th "	5th "	Albany	20th "	22nd "
Colombo	12th "	16th "	Freemantle	23rd "	26th "
Singapore	21st "	23rd "	Mauritius	4th Aug	8th Aug
Albany	3rd May	4th May	Durban	13th "	15th "
Melbourne	6th "	18th "	Simonstown	18th "	23rd "
Sydney	20th "	24th "	St Vincent	3rd Sep	5th Sep
Hawkesbury Rr.	24th "	27th "	Quebec	15th "	21st "
Sydney	27th "	6th Jun	Halifax	23rd Sep	21st Oct
			St Johns	23rd Oct	25th "

"H.M.S. OPHIR"

OUTWARD · BOUND.

"H.M.S. DIADEM." OUR · FIRST · ESCORT "H.M.S. NIOBE"

Discription of the Ophir.

The leading particulars. are. length over all 482ᶠᵗ beam 52ᶠᵗ6ᴵᴺ. depth 37ᶠᵗ) gross register 6910 ᵀᴺˢ) Horse power 10.000. (engines. two. independant triple ex (boilers seven)(working pressure 160 lls)(speed 18. ᴷᴺᴼᵀˢ)

Commisioned at Tilbury docks 26ᵗʰ ᶠᴱᴮ/01, with a compliment of 125 bluejackets., 100 marines, 37 bandsmen, 20 boys, 7 engineer officers, 88 stokers, 2 pursers, 50 stewards, 9 cooks & assistant cooks, 3 bakers, 2 butchers, 1 laundry man. and wife, 1 printer, 2 barbers, The whole under the command of Commodore A.L. Winsloe. and 21 other officers. to take "H.R.H. the Duke. and Duchess of Cornwall & York," on their colonial tour. The ships compliment with the royal suite included would be about 525 all told.

⟶ ◦◦◦◦◦

Left Tilbury docks the 27 of Febuary 1901 & ajusted compasses off "Sheerness," We then proceeded to "Portsmouth," arriving there the following morning, and anchored at "Spithead" in thick fog; which delayed our going up harbour; which we did about midday; and went alongside the south railway, or farewell jelly as it is called, and in the afternoon prepared for coaling, the next day we took in several hundreds of tons. of best hand picked coal. Two remarkable features of the coaling was first the absence of dirt and dust greatley due to the manner in which the ship was protected by coaling screens; and secondly the we where coaled by people from shore; the likes of which I had never seen done in home waters before. The next day we started taking in government stores. Nothing happened concerning us until the 8th of March when we witnessed the departure of our escort the "St George & Juno." for "Suez" the first named having on board two royal steam barges; On the 11th the royal yacht "Victoria & Albert" was berthed alongside the jetty astern of us. The day following was visited by "Lord Selborne" first lord of the admiralty, 15th "The King. Queen. Duke. Dutchess". ect arrived. The next day the "King" confered the Victorian Order on the men belonging to the guard of honour that rendered such valuable assistance. at "Windsor" at the time of the burial of our late beloved "Queen Victoria"; after which he distributed medals to men from "S. Africa". "The King" then came on board and inspected us. and then lunched with the "Duke & Duchess. Commodore". ect. About 4.30 in the evening we cast off from the jetty and proceeded slowly down the harbour, preceeded first by the "Trinity House yacht" and next by the "Alberta" with the "King and Queen" on board; eight torpedo boat destroyers in two lines one off each quarter brought up the rear; immence crowds of people lined the shores on both sides, and one could see handkerchiefs waving as far as the eye could reach, whilst several bands could be heard playing; and above all the cheers of the multitude both on shore and on the many boats which accompanied us out of the harbour. The "Alberta" still kept right ahead, till well out at "Spithead"; when she slowed down and dropped abrest of us. We then manned the rigging; and the commander. called for three cheers for the "King & Queen" which where heartily given, the "Duke. & Duchess" on the fore bridge waving. adiew he with cap; she with handkerchief. The "Alberta's crew then gave us us three cheers, We then gave three more cheers, went full speed ahead and we soon left the "Alberta" far astern. Our first escort the "Diadem & Niobe". then took up their positions one off each quarter; and we proceeded down channel, en-route for "Gibralta." When we got fairly out at sea, the sea proved to be very moderate, only a gentle heaving of the ship to remind you that you where at sea. The next day Sunday a little rain fell, and we went to church in the Royal dining saloon, a magnificently decorated apartment the Duke was there, but the Duchess did not make her appearance; in fact nothing had been seen of her since the evening before. after divine service we where served out with a little souvenir! a small testament; with a print of the "Duke & Duchess" & children for a front ispiece; about 4 O.Clock in the evening the Duchess sent a box of shamrock on the mens messdeck with her compliments, and being the 17 of old "Ireland" every man went to evening quarters with a spray in his cap. All went well the next day untill about 10 O.Clock in the first watch when the wind began to blow. and the sea to rise; and by midnight it was blowing half a gale, and we where tumbling about in a heavy sea, one of the hydraulic cranes got adrift and smashed our upper fore and aft bridge; we shipped large quantities of water but taking her all: together the "Ophir" proved a good sea boat. The landlubbers had a very bad time and swore they would go back home when they reached Gib; but the sea moderated a good deal by the following evening, and the Duchess came on deck; the first we had seen of her since we started. The next morning we sighted the Rock; and as we got closer we saw that the whole of the channel fleet was drawn up in two lines. manned & dressed. When about ¼ a mile off the Majestic started to salute followed by the whole squadron it was a grand sight; and as we passed between the lines each ships company gave us three ringing cheers; and their bands played the King. We dropped anchor inside the **Mole** and got out the royal pulling barge, and two steam cutters. Between our ship and the landing place; was stretched two lines of 12 oared cutters. At noon the Duke left the ship in the royal barge, and she looked very nice as she passed between the lines of cutters their crews standing bare headed each officer saluting; soon after his return to the ship in the evening the whole fleet illuminated; and I only make a poor show of it in the picture below.

Channel Fleet at Gibralta

The Duke went ashore again the following day; and in the evening the fleet again illuminated the rock itself was illuminated; also the Portuguese warship, Snt Gabriel but the Spanish ship Infanta ISABEL, took no part whatever in the celebrations; we prepared for sea. The next morning turned out nice and fine, and at half past nine we got up anchor J. and proceeded out of harbour, and it made one feel proud to belong to such a nation as we steamed slowly through the stately lines of flag bedecked warships, and cheer after cheer echoed across the sunlit waters.

SAN. GABRIEL
PORTUGUESE

INFANTA ISABEL
SPANISH

The Magnificent again started to salute, the remainder following suit, after which we turned our ships head for Malta, signalled down the engine room for full speed, and with our second escort the Andromeda & Diana following in our wake; soon left the historic rock far behind, we then signalled for our escort to go on ahead. The day turned out to be the finest we had had since we left England and by midday it was quite hot. The following day we left of gurnseys and wore white capcovers. On our Starboard beam the coast of Africa showed up quite plain. Sunday morning we sighted the Thetis British cruiser and she signaled Bothers conditions of surrender. We went to Church in the Royal Saloon again; and the service went off much better but the Duchess was still unable to attend, in the evening we slowed down. Monday morn early we sighted Malta; and before long we perceived a number of craft approaching, which proved to be destroyers painted white; and they made a splendid spectacle as they bounded over the dark blue waters, thundering out a royal salute with their 12 pdrs as the came on in two lines in an opposite direction to us, one line passing down each side of us, and they put one in mind of a shoal of porpoises, as they leapt and plunged through the water; when they got astern they altered course 16 points and again passed us, and took up their positions one of each bow and in this formation we entered the harbour. The noise now became deffening as over forty men-of-war began to salute; (its puts me in mind of Parde burg) I heard a man say, a man who had served with the Naval Brigade in S.Africa. The shore from the beach to the top of the bastions was thronged with the teeming population both of Malta & Goza, and cheer after cheer reechoed from height to height, it was a splendid welcome and showed that the Maltese are quite happy under the Union Jack. We made fast head and stern to two buoys in the center of the Grand Harbour; and the water police had their work cut out to keep back the hundreds of boats or Dycoes as they are commonly called here. The "Duke & Duchess" went ashore in the royal pulling barge about midday. The shore being lined with soldiers, the Navy being stationed from the "Opera house" in "Strada Reale" to Spencers Monument

DESTROYERS ESCORTING US INTO MALTA HARBOUR

The whole fleet again saluted during the passage ashore. When their Royal Highnesses landed they looked as happy as possible, and beaming over with good humour and smiles, graciously returned the salutations of the people, and all along the route nothing but happy and joyous faces, stretched forward to catch a glimse of the illustrious son of Our King. Floriana of course was a foretaste of the reception in Valletta the houses and streets being decorated in handsome style. We all know that Valletta redily adapts itself to decoration, there is a quaintness and old time feeling about the houses, which modern cities never offer. Even without decoration Valletta is quaint picturesque and romantic, but when to its usual charms are added decorated and ever greened venetian masts, banners and flags by the hundreds flying in the breeze, beautiful triumphal arches, pavements thronged with a loyal picturesque and enthusiastic crowd, the road way lined with soldiers in Karki and Bluejackets in strawhats, and last but not least, the balconies and windows filled with visions of feminine beauty and loveliness, the world-famed Strada Reale presents a scene which no other town in Europe can furnish. Their Royal Highnesses visited the palace and inspected the guard of honour there, afterwards proceeded up to the Royal Balcony facing the main guard, to witness the forces detailed from the Navy & Army to march past. Upwards of 6000 men defiled past the Royal Balcony in gallant style. The march past over their Royal Highnesses lunched with His Excellency the governor at the Palace, their Royal Highnesses subsiquently returned to the Ophir about midnight. 27th of March the day of departure was a very event full one, and even early in the morning, one could see preperations going on and as the evening drew on, weird looking craft began to make their appearence on the water, most of them resembling animals & birds, the best products being a swan & whale, the Elephant Crocodile Seaserpent Lion Camel & Dragon being very good; At eight pm, as by magic the whole fleet illuminated

Aquatic
Display at
Malta

and in the background 500 starrockets ascended simultaniously; the harbour now presented a sight the likes of which I had never seen before

All round the harbour coloured lamps could be seen outlining the old battlements and bastions, whilst along the sea front the Maltese had made a grand show every window door gable ect being festuned. with coloured lamps, but it was on the water that all eyes where fixed; apart from the fleet the Ophir was also illuminated and the weird craft; the dragons, & sea serpent kept up a continous rain of fire and smoke from their mouths in the shape of all manner of fireworks, Lined up along side both sides of the harbour, outside the fleet where the destroyers, their searchlights crossing over us, and making an arch

H.M.S ANDROMEDA.   H.M.S. DIANA.

way reaching to the sky. About half past nine another flight of 500 rockets ascended, and at midnight a grand salvo of a thousand rockets was the signal for us to depart. As we slipped the buoy, the forts began to salute, and all the steamers kept up a continual din with their hooters And as we slowly passed down the harbour between the thousands of boats the ones on the starboard hand burnt green port fires, and on the port side they used red ones, whilst the people cheered them selves hoarse

......«««« MALTA'S SONG OF WELCOME »»»».......

THEY COME, OUR HOPE FROM ALBIONS SHORES AFAR,
TO NAME OF AGE A RACE NEATH SOUTHERN STAR;
AND NATIONS, ENVIOUS, MARK THEIR STEEL CLAD TRAIN,
STRETCHING, IMPERIOUS, LEAGUES ACROSS THE MAIN.
BUT LO! WE HAIL THE LAND WITH PROMISE GREAT
SELF-STRONG PROCLAIMED WITH POMP BY PARENT STATE
AND VITAL ORGAN OF THE EMPIRE'S HEART
IN GREATNESS GROWN WITH EACH EXPANDING PART.
LOUD IN AUSTRALIA'S JOY, WITH HEART AND VOICE
TO ALL THE WORLD, WE CRY, THAT WE REJOICE

THEN DECK THE TOWN OF LA VALLETTE,
WITH FLAG, AND FLOWER, AND FAIRY LAMP.
LET JOYOUS HEARTS NEW JOY BEGET
WITH HUM OF THRONG, AND MARTIAL TRAMP
AT SIGHT OF GLIDING CARNIVAL
OF CRAFT WEIRD BRIGHT FANTASTICAL
AT SHOWER OF STARS OF PAINTED LIGHT, AT MUSIC'S THRILL, AT CANNON'S ROAR
REECHOING FROM THE BASTIONED HEIGHT THAT SPURNED THE TURK FROM MALTA'S SHORE

MALTE BOAT

MALTESE CROSS

HOLY STONE

SUEZ. CANAL.
COMPANIES. OFFICES.

It was a grand send off and no mistake, and though I had been working on deck for nearly twentyfour hours, I forgot fatigue and was lost in wonder. When wegot outside we found the Diana waiting for us, so we extingwished our illuminations, and turned our ships head for Port Said, the lights of the fleet being visable for some considerable time. The Andromeda remained behind to pickup mails, but she caught us up the following day, The next morning the sky became overcast, and remained so until the following evening when it began to rain. We run into Port Said, about half past four, passing a P&O liner and they cheered us as wepassed; we made fast opposite the Pilot House and prepared for coaling; the Duke & Duchess made an official Visit about 5..30. and inspected a company of the 2nd Scudenesse. returned to the ship soon after 6- p.m.. We started coaling about 10. pm, and it was like a babel to hear the incessant chanting and gibberish chatter of the natives, by 4 next morning all our coal was inboard, and by six we where under weigh and steaming slowly down the Seuz Canal, followed by a pilot tug it was a very pleasant trip through the canal, but the weather was changing rapidly; getting hotter and hotter, now we would pass a caravan, and then a croud of Arab boys, who would run along the banks crying out for buiscuit, as far as the eye could reach on either side streat the sandy desert and when we

S.T. TITAN
ESCORTING US
THROUGH THE
SUEZ CANAL

came across a "Bringing to Station" with its few shrubs and palms the green was quite refreshing to the sight, At Ismalia we came across the Britannic and we found out that she carried a number of homeward troops, from Australia, and as we passed them they gave us three rousing cheers; which we returned with equal energy, our band then played Home sweet home & Auld lang syne, and it was peculiar how these familiar tunes touched our feelings, although we had only just left home. We dropped anchor in the evening in the Bitter lakes, and proceeded on our way first thing in the morning. passing two liners one a German; and one belonging to the same line as the Ophir. We arrived at Suez about 10 in the forenoon, and the Hussar a British gunboat saluted us, we anchored, but got up anchor again and proceeded on our way and at midday. We had a rather uneventfull voyage through the Red

GUARD SHIP   SUEZ

sea, except that we met the Cocatrice a British sloop and she signalled a great capture of men stores and cutte by French. We passed through the Gates of Hell about midnight on friday, and arrived at Aden the following morn, where we met with our old acquaintances the Snr George & Juno, and the Snr George had one of the Royal steam boats out ready for use; as far as we could see from the ship.

H.M.S. HUSSAR.

Aden was entirely devoid of vegetation, nothing but rugged Vandyke brown coloured mountains surrounding the town, but the sea front and some parts of the town was very prettily decorated; their Royal Highnesses went ashore about 4 in the afternoon and returned about 7 in the evening. The Duke also gave orders for the Racoon gunboat to pay off; and she instantly hoisted the paying off pendant—

"HMS. COCATRICE"

In the evening the town illuminated as well as could be expected considering that they have only the primative methods of light. The Egypt a stately liner also illuminated; so, did one or two other yatch's that lay in harbour; Whilst the Racoon had a design picked out in electric light; a crown under lined with a letter G and M representing the christian names of their Royal Highnesse's. A reception was given on board about nine for all the big nobs of the place including officers and wives of the troops stationed

H.M.S. Racoon at Aden

here; but every one was out of the ship by 11. pm and by half past we where under weigh, together with our escort. and bound for Colombo. Our trip to Colombo was not very eventfull except that a concert was given in the grand saloon and considering it was organised in very quick time; it was a

RED HAIRED NIGGER ADEN

NATIVE BOAT ADEN

complete success, what had a lot to do with it was we had a complete set of theatrical costumes, supplied by the court costumers, London. I give a programe of the events on the next page. The weather now was very hot, and most men where in a

continual sweat from morn till night, during the day lots
of life was to be seen, shoals of flying fish, dolphin's, ect could
be seen every where, some of them quite close. to the ship. We
arrived at Colombo early friday morning, and found it to
be a very beautifull place, with waving palms, and scyamore
more. stretching a way for miles; whilst
in the far distance was, a range of mountains
hardley visable. The, town itself was
decorated every where, as well as all
the ships and boats in the harbour, prominent
amongst them being Liptons boats with a
great show of Irish ensigns flying. Their
Royal Highnesses went ashore at 1.pm
amidst the usual ceremony of salutes
after looking round Colombo, they proceeded

HMS OPHIR"
PROGRAME

1. BANJO SOLO ..... S.B.S. WHYBREW
2. Comic Song. It'll take a lot of that _ 2nd P.O. HOWE
3. SONG - - - - - - - - - - LORD. CRICHTON
4. SONG _ So fare The well _ Mc A.E. WAKEFORD.
5. COSTER Song. Mrs Carter. Bombr KELLY R.M.A.
6. COMIC. Song. Haul me back again SgT MANLY R.M.A.
7. SONG _ Twin duet _ Lieut MAITLAND & Mc BRYER.
8. SONG _ The Diver _ GUNNER COWLING. R.M.A.
9. DANCE - - - - - - - - - Log Sea Silvie
10. Coon Song Is yer mammy allways wid yer. PRICE
P.O. 2nd C?

GOD SAVE THE KING

April 10th 1902

PROGRAME OF FIRST CONCERT

by train to Kandi, inspecting the native troops. and presenting
the Ceylon mounted infantry, with the Kings Colours and South African
war medals, the also witnessed some native dancing, snake charming
ect. The crew of the Ophir had a grand feed of fruit, pineapple,
bannana's, mangoes ect here, they where also invited to a feast
ashore but they did not go on account of coaling ship. The Planters
association also sent off several hundred pound cases of tea for
the ships crew, What amused me most here was the niggers
six or seven of them would come off to the ship on the trunk
a cocoanut tree; and standing up, would sing Ta-rara-boom-dea
making a smacking noise with the upper part of their arms against
the body, as an accompanyment, after which they would ask for
you to throw in money, for which they would dive like fish

seldom loseing the coin. The boats here are very curious being less than a foot in breadth, and kept from capsizing by means of an outrigger, or log of wood secured to two poles sticking out from the side of the boat, these boats are called Cattermerans

TA.RA.RA. BOOM. DE AY.

I went ashore Monday afternoon and found a great difference to any other place I had ever visited; 999 out of a thousand were blacks, and hardly one dressed the same, some with long hair some short, some with a pate shining like metal, in fact every design imagine able was used in dressing the hair, but the majority had it done up behind like a woman's. Nearly every one glided noiselessly about without shoes, and the beauty and richness of their appearel surprised me, some of the better class wearing dresses together with jewelry, worth many thousands of pounds. In the evening, we, together with the three ships of the East Indies squadron, and

COLOMBO
SCAVENGER
CROW

most of the merchant men in harbour illuminated, and about half past 10, their Royal Highnesses and suite returned to the ship. About 8 in the morning the East Indies squadron together with our escort, went out of harbour and Admiral Bainbridge carried out steam tatics until half

H.M.S. "HIGHFLYER."

H.M.S. "POMONE."

H.M.S. "MARATHON."

"East Indies Squadron"

past nine, when we slowly steamed round the breakwater carefully picking our way amongst the swarms of native boats, and whilst the forts boomed out a Royal salute the St. George and Juno took up their position in single line off our starboard quarter, and the Highflier and Pomone off the port quarter, and in this formation we proceeded on our way to Singapore. In the evening about 5 O.clock the whole of us hove to, and sent whatever mails we had to the Pomone, and when she had them all she left and being a very fast boat she was soon hull down. The Highflier meanwhile had steamed right round us and then came close up to us, her crew manned the rigging and they they gave us three hearty cheers, cheer such as only British seamen can give, we then gave three cheers for the Admiral, the Highflier then sheared off, the Juno then took up her position of the Port quarter and once more we proceeded on our way, nothing of interest taking place untill about 11 O.clock the first watch on Wednesday night when we caught a proper tropical shower

A Tropical Shower.

In these latitudes at this time of the year, it lightens incessantly, but to night the flashes where of extra brilliancy, showing in three or four places in the sky at once, not a breath of wind stirred the indigo waters and after a flash of lightening more vivid than any of the preceeding ones, a rumble of distant thunder shook the stillness, accompanied directley after by a rush off wind accompanied with extra large spots of rain, instantly the boson's mate roared, "close all ventalation," and then the fun began. A terrific crash of thunder broke overhead, and shook the ship throughout, and the lightening played with such dazzling brilliancy that our escort could be seen as plain as in broard daylight, although they where a mile away; and down came the rain, came down I say, I guess it was chucked down; it put me in mind as if the sea had been taken up to the clouds and then dropped in a lump; it was impossible to see now, the rain came with such force, in fact it was just the same as if a fire hose was being played full in the face, I believe the rain found its way into every part of the ship the Royal compartments suffering; but it was soon over, and a few minutes after the ship was quite dry, and in the distance the lightening played feebley. The following Saturday was kept as a Sunday, and early Sunday morn we ran into Singapore a very pretty, but, low lying, well wooded place, and went alongside the jetty and after their Royal Highnesses had departed commenced coaling at once, the coal was got in by Chinamen and they kept up a continual run all the day long, their

CHINESE. COAL HEAVERS

pecularity being to run when loaded and walk with empty baskets We finished coaling about 5 in the evening and steamed round to the man.of.war anchorage, and anchored. Here we found. The Aurora. Arethusa Linnet. Rosario. Algerine.

belonging to the British China Squadron, also a Dutchman a Frenchman and an Italian man of war. The following morning a horde of Chinese painters came aboard and gave us a complete coat of paint out side, which made us look

"H.M.S. RASARIO,"   "H.M.S. ALGERINE,"   "H.M.S. AURORA."

a little more respectable than we had been for some time. On the next day a sad incident occured; a stoker who had been ill some few days, suddenly died of disentry, and after consulting the Commudore it was decided that he should be burried at sea the same evening. To day was also a regetta for the natives

"FRENCH"   "DUTCH"   "ITALIAN"

and a verry pretty sight it was, expecrally the sailing races with the crews dressed in every colour imagineable There was also two or three Malay war canoes, which must have been terrors in the earlier history of this place. They raced round and round our ship time after time, keeping

" "MALAY WAR CANOE"

up a continual din with their Tom-Toms, and every now and then giving vent to their feelings by an unearthly yell; a large number of natives came off in canoes; or at least logs of wood not much larger than themselves, hollowed out, and as fast as they filled with water they forced it out with a

H.M.S. ARETHUSA.

peculiar motion of the feet, these men where far superior to those at Colombo, in diving for money. In the afternoon their Royal Highness came on board loaded with presents from the loyal natives, including a pair of Siameese kittens., named Rajar & Ranie. As soon as everything was on board. We got up anchor and admidst the Thunder of the guns of all the men of war in the harbour we slowly steamed down the Sunda or at least the Mallacca Straits the S.t George & Juno following. We had only been under-weigh an hour or so when we sighted two men-o-war right

H.M.S. LINNET.

MALAY. VILLIAGE

ahead, which proved to be two Japanese battleships and as they drew alongside our starboard side they both saluted and the S^{nt} George returned it. Just before

evening quarters
the fore topmen
had orders to lay
the port foremost
upper ladder flat.
this was the first
thing towards the
funeral of our ship

JAPANESE. BATTLESHIP.S

mate who only died the same morning; the seamen ect where only wearing duck trousers and flannels because of the heat of the tropics, but the bo-sons mate piped all men will attend divisions with their jumpers on; after divisions, the seamen and marines where marched on the promenade deck and fell in with with an open space reach

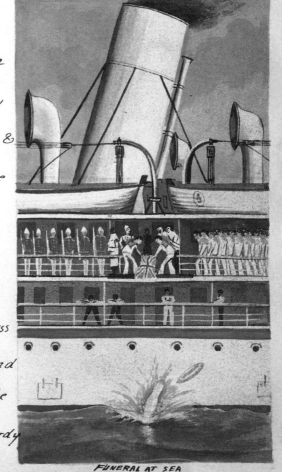

ing from forward aft. between them, and each man was served out with a prayer & hymn book; the little noise the men where making, was quickly hushed, when the strains of Chopin's funeral march came softly from aft; Walking up the space between the men, came the stokers and mess mates of deceased; preceeded by the band then came the Rev. Wood. followed by the corpse borne on the shoulders of sir sturdy

FUNERAL AT SEA

stokers; as the mornful posession slowly passed up the avenue of soldiers, sailors, and marines; I noticed that several men where very much affected, the possesion stopped and the corpse was placed on the upper part of the ladder already mentioned Over the body was placed a Union Jack, and on top was a beautiful wreath of white roses and maden-hair fern. presented by Her Royal Highness the Duchess. The silence now was painfull but was relieved some-what when the RerWood began the funeral service and a loud splash followed the words commit his body to the deep; and as I glanced over the side all I could see was a shattered wreath floating on the the troubled waters A firing party of marines now fired three volleys over the spot, and then all hands joined in the hymn; A few more years shall roll, very softly at first but towards the end it gathered strength; and enabled most of those present to relieve their feelings in song; the Duchess and most of the ladies and gentlemen present seemed very much

CHINESE. JUNK.

affected right through the ceremony. expecially those that where roving the seas for the first time. About 9-30, the following evening a terrible voice, coming from over the bows, roared Ship— Ahoy, a pause and then the same trumpet like voice continued, what ship is that, and wither bound, what cargo, ect. The officer on watch instantly replied, His

Britannic Majesties Yatch Ophir, bound for Australia, with their Royal Highnesses, the Duke & Duchess of Cornwall & York on board; the voice then answered, "As a messenger from old King Neptune, I bid you welcome to his domains; and he bids me to say that he will pay the ship a visit to morrow with his wife and all his court," the officer on the bridge again spoke, but no answer came back, no sound but the rush of water from our bows, as we plowed our way across the Indian ocean The next morning all was bustle and activity, all hands being employed rigging up a huge bath in which father Neptune was to baptise all the new entries entrusted to his care, namely; all those that had never crossed the line before, The navigator now said that we where rapidly nearing the line

CROSSING THE LINE

It was about ten O.Clock the following morn, when old Neptune came aboard, making his appearence in a chariot composed of huge sea shells, the raw jagged edges edged with rope that had the appearence of belonging to some ship of a bygone age. Upon reaching the promenade deck, three representative one of Britannia one Australia and one Canada, stepped into the chariot. and then the whole lot glided for-ward drawn by the Guard of honour; composed of the biggest marines in the ship, and dressed in all the outlandish costumes possible

I noticed that all the ladies and gentlemen belonging to the Royal suite, where very busy with their cameras. When Neptune accompanied by his wife and the whole of his court reached the fore end of the deck, close to the large tank; he was received by their Royal Highnesses the Duke and Duchess; after a few words of greeting. Neptune stepped from his charriot and carrying a silver goblet in his hand, walked up to the Duchess and sprinkled water on her head, saying at the same time It makes me feel most happy, in the name of Salt water, to christen you Queen of the Seas; Ampitrite then stepped forward and presented the Duchess with a bouquet of coral

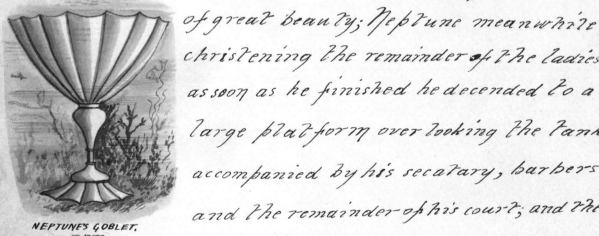

NEPTUNE'S GOBLET.

of great beauty; Neptune meanwhile christening the remainder of the ladies as soon as he finished he decended to a large platform over looking the tank accompanied by his secatary, barbers and the remainder of his court; and then the ball opened. His secatary unrolled a large parchment and read out the roll of Greenhorns and Goshens, beginning with the Duke himself; the Duke instantly stepped forward, and seated himself in the chair placed at the very edge of the platform over looking the canvas tank, and was instantly seized by Neptunes barbers and duly lathered and scraped in the orthodox stile, and then pitched head over heels into the tank, where he recieved his babtism at the hands of the sea bears

in the Tank, who gave him a severe ducking, admidst the
laughter of the Duchess, and suite, and the whole of the
assembled ships company; but no time could be lost, and the
Secetary instantly called out the next one to be babtised

NEPTUNE, HIS WIFE, AND CHILDREN.

and then the next, and so on, each officer and man suffering
according to his popularity, some where litterally lathered from
head to foot with the vile compound Old Neptune's barbers used

COMING EVENT
CAST THEIR
SHADOWS BEFORE

and then nearly drowned in the Tank; and woe be to the man
that attempted to remonstrate; if he opened his mouth it was instantly
filled up with lather from a large syringe deftly used by Neptunes

physician and if violent was soon passified by the Guard of honour, one of them being the Champion heavy weight lifter of the Navy and Army. The fun was now at its height, and to increase it a stiff breeze sprang up from South.west, bringing with it an heavy swell, which made the water in the tank like unto a tempestious sea, and washed baptised and baptisers about like corks; towards the end of the ceremony one of the men whilst being flung into the tank, managed to bring one of the barbers with him And another whose feelings where hurt by rough usage made a desperate charge and shoved the heavy weight-lifter in on top of him, then dozens of bluejackets joined in the general melee, when all of a sudden one side of the tank collapsed and washed the whole lot down the waterways, and when they where gathered up; Neptune, Amphitrite and the whole of his court had dissapeared, gone, but not forgotten, To day was the 25ᵗᵈ of April, and already the weather was rapidly getting colder and the sea, and sky, resuming that leaden colour so often seen round the coast of England, on the 29ᵗᵈ we ran away from our escort and the following night we ran into Albany in the province of Western Australia; and

ALBATROSS

landed Sir Arthur Lawley, the govenor of this province; as he left the ship, the ships company gave three hearty cheers

We left early the following morning, as we passed out by one entrance, we perceived our old friends the "S.^{nt} George and Juno" creeping in by another; It was now quite as cold as when we left England, and large numbers of those gigantic sea birds called Albratross's followed day and night in our wake, it was most bewitching to watch these mighty birds; for hours they would keep up with the ship without a motion of the wings, skimming along as if secured to the ship by a line, now and then with the tips of their huge wings dipped an inch or so in the water. On the 5th of May we dropped anchor off Snapper Point, about 30 or 40 ^{m<u>es</u>} from Melbourne; here Lord Hope town paid us a visit, and dined with their Royal Highnesses. As we approached this place, we where met by four ships of the Australian Squadron, the Royal Arthur flagship, and the Ringarooma, Wallaroo, Mildura, and also our old chum

PART OF THE
AUSTRALIAN
SQUADRON

ROYAL ARTHUR
RINGAROOMA
WALLAROO
MILDURA

the Juno; followed an hour or so afterwards by the S.^{nt} George, they all dropped anchor with us here; the next morning we all proceeded on our way to Melbourne, the Ophir leading; About half 10 in the fore noon we sighted a gigantic Russian warship off our starboard bow, looking bigger still in the morning mist, which the sun had not yet dispersed, next we sighted a Yankee Cruiser, Then a

Netherlands cruiser, and finally two German cruisers
Just before we dropped anchor; the whole of the warships
both British and Foreign opened fire in a Royal salute;
and as the Sun was now rapidly clearing away the mist,
a brilliant scene presented itself to our view. We dropped
anchor about midday, and were soon.
surrounded by pleasure steamers, or
hurrah boats as they called on account
of the amount of cheering their
passengers indulge in,
and the sun shone out
brilliantly welcome
ing us to the fair
land of
Australia

Our Stay in Australia

MELBOURNE

Their Royal Highnesses went ashore about 2 in the afternoon
in a beautifull paddle steamer the "Hygeia," accompanied
by the whole of their suite, and met with a splendid
reception at the St. Kilda pier. Under the cloudless sky
the St. Kilda pier was a very pretty sight. It's great length
was emphasised by a crimson carpet, running along the centre
from end to end, and rows of masts, from which flew brightly

colored pennants, the shelter shed was made quite beautiful. Midway was a handsome arch, erected by the St. Kilda yacht men, and at the place of landing, a canopy which was festooned and draped. Never before was the pier such a centre of attraction. The Esplanade and its stands were thronged with people, and every window commanding a view of the scene was occupied. Then on the bay side, was the Royal Yacht "Ophir"

St KILDA AND PRAHRAN ARCH

and all the British and Foreign men of war, with a background of white smoke, the remnant of the Royal salute they had thundered out during the passage of the Royal party from ship to shore. The pier was lined on both sides by the Victorian Permanent Artillery, and the 1st battalion Infantry Brigade. It was just 5 minutes to 2 when the Royal visitors walked down the gangway from the "Hygeia," and were received by His Excellency the Governor-General. This was the signal for loud and continued cheers of welcome from the immence crowds of enthusiastic Britishers & Colonials

I will now leave their Royal Highnesses, as every one must be familliar with the enthusiastic reception the loyal Australians gave to the eldest son and daughter in law of our most noble King. I will now try and describe the way in which Melbourne was decorated in honour of the great event. In the first place Melbourne is a fine city in itself

CHINEE ARCH   DUKE'S ARCH

and add to it decorations far surpassing any thing we have ever attempted in England it presented a magnificent sight. Triumphial arches that presented as good a spectical by day as by night, & illuminated fountains, All the principal houses and shops were illuminated from chimney to doorstep. Mirriads of banners flags and streamers, and last but not least a teeming population of "Britishers" to the back bone, who where every ready to pass a cheering remark, or give a harty slap on the back of any jolly tar they passed, especially if he belonged to the "Ophir." In the afternoon after the Duke and Duchess had landed we placed the Ophir along

side one of the piers, and we where shortly followed by the St George
and Juno; and then the Australian ships followed suit. The next day
we started to coal and about midday the hugh Russian cruiser and
the American cruiser took up their positions alongside one of the piers next
to us. Port watch went on sixty hours leave the next day and came
back with wonderfull stories of how good the people had been to them

RUSSIAN CRUISER GROMOBOI   U.S.S. BROOKLYN

On friday evening my own watch (starboard) went on their
sixty hours leave, Of course the city itself lay about 3 miles

POPULAR AUSTRALIAN FLAGS

from the seafront and we went up by train, and I soon noticed
that the carriages where much better fitted up than those
in the old country. When we arrived at Melbourne we where

surprised to hear that we where to travel free of charge. As I walked out of the station, I was at once filled with amazement at the beauty of the scene which presented itself to my astonished gaze, each side of the wide streets

GERMAN. CRUISER. HANSA.

as far as the eye could reach, was one mass of coloured bunting and silk; tall and gaily festuned venetian masts. running from end to end, interrupted only by a triumphal arch here and there. Each arch had a name the Chinese arch was built by the Chinese, and was very picturesque; A most novel arch was the one built entirely of boxes of butter, representing the daily amount of butter exported from this place; the design being a Norman gateway; The Queen arch was of very original design, but I dont think it proved the success the designer thought it would. The King arch was grand, and very much admired, the Dukes arch was very

much on the same scale and colouring. The city and the

citizens arch where magnificent structures of ancient

Roman design; in fact they where all very good and it is

impossible for me to put all I saw and heard into this

BUTTER ARCH   KINGS. ARCH.

book, but all this show was nothing compared with the people

they where grand and no mistake, even without an exception

and its true when I say that I was treated better than if

GERMAN. CORVETT   H. M COLONIAL. SHIP CEREBOS   DUTCH CRUISER

I was at home with relations and friends, it did not matter

which way one turned, you met with a cheering remark though

I must say that the "Ophir's" came in for the greatest share

of the good feeling the people displayed. and I assure you

it was with a feeling of deep regret that I returned to the ship. On the afternoon that I returned to the ship it was open to visitors and I shall never forget the immence crowds that continually came and went, it was a regular crush on board but the best of good feeling prevailed, the bluejackets doing everything they could for their guests as I may call them, and as the evening drew on a space we had our work cut out to get the ship, cleared thousands of them remained on the pier alongside the ship. At eight 6.Clock exact, every man-of-war burst forth into light, and although I have seen a lot of naval illuminations I can safely say that these where the best I had ever seen, and gentle reader dont be offended when I say that the Foreign men-of-war beat us hollow in the way they dressed their ships; but bear in mind that they must have spent a great deal of time and trouble in getting ready, whilst our ships where at drill, and getting ready for something more serious than illuminating ship. But the British boys in blue where not to be done and nearly all our ships companies made up an extempor concert on the upper deck; which amused the crowds on the jetty immensely. The following morning we heard that our programe was to be altered; Their Royal Highnesses where going to Brisbane by train, as there was a slight attack of plague at the place, and if they made their visit by the sea the "Ophir" would have to go into quarantine for perhaps a fortnight; which would have altogether upset more important engagements. So on saturday the 18th of May, about midday it was with a heavy heart that we cast off from the pier; amidst the cheers, waving of handkerchiefs, ect of the many kind friends we had made in the fair city of "Melbourne", and steamed

H.M.S. St. GEORGE.

out past the foreign men-of-war on our way to "Sydney", Our escort comprising the St. George only. We arrived at "Sydney" on Monday morning and were at once struck with the magnificence of the harbour, As yet very little had been done in the manner of decoration; the following morning we went in dock, and had our bottom scraped and painted; came out again the following day and went alongside the coaling warf at garden island, and took in a very large quantity of coal: On friday we left for the Hawksbury river, to embark Their Royal Highnesses. arriving there the middle of the day, this river has been most appropreately named the "Australian .Rhine", as its beauties are of the best and rarest . . The next day their Royal Highnesses arrived by the stern weel steamer the Captain Cook; or at least the General Gardon, I should say, and escorted by the Captain Cook, Their Royal Highnesses did not look much the worse for their prolonged stay on shore The next day the Royal party had a delightful picnic up the river

STERN WHEEL. STEAMER GENERAL GORDON.

in the "General Gordon," when they returned I noticed that the captain of the boat was in the seventh heaven of delight at the honour, I suppose of taking the Duke and Duchess for the trip, and he left us an happy man, with a present from the Duke I don't know what it was; to day was the Duchess's birthday and the ships dressed rainbow fashion and fired a salute

In the evening the Duchess sent word to the men that they could drink her health on her birthday; rum was served out on the upper deck, and both the Duke and Duchess had a tot of Navy Rum too, The Duke then stepped foreward and said he had been asked by the Duchess to thank the ships company for their kind wishes for her birthday; The whole ships company then gave three ringing cheers, and the band played god bless the "Prince of Wales." A most laughable incident now occured, one man started to sing; She's a jolly good fellow, and the whole ships company took it up and gave it lip, the Duchess seemed greatly amused, the men then gave three more cheers, and then spliced the main brace in true nautical style I may here mention that this was the second time we spliced the main brace, the first time being at the Dukes invitation the day we crossed the line, The next day we got up anchor, and made for "Sydney", As soon as we got outside, we where met by the Australian fleet, who saluted us and then took up their positions astern of our escort the St George & Juno.

Sydney

THE HEADS

The sun shone forth brilliantly as we passed between the

Heads. The most prominent points where thronged with people and there was plenty of waving handkerchiefs, but very little cheering, as we slowly made our way up the beautiful harbour of Sydney; Numbers of pleasure steamers of a distinct yankee pattern, and thronged with people, came and met us; As we got closer to the town, we found another portion of the Australian squadron there, and also the huge Russian Cruiser from "Melbourne;" who at once saluted us, together with the shore batteries; it was in the midst of all this din that we made fast to a buoy in "Farm Cove," opposite "Government House" and close to a small island which used to be of great use for the safe keeping of prisoners in the days of transportation. It was about 2-p-m when their Royal Highnesses went ashore; dense crowds of spectators surrounded the landing place, The

ROYAL, PULLING BARGE

Royal pulling barge conveyed their Royal Highnesses from the Ophir to the shore, where they met with a hearty reception, and then drove to Government House by a roundabout rout so, as to view the decorations. Starboard

watch, my own, went on sixty hours leave in the evening, and
when I went ashore, I met with a great dissappoint, I expected
to find Sydney like Melbourne, but there was no comparison;
not only where the streets narrow and badley paved; but
the decorations where very meagre; in fact it was an
insult to call them decorations at all; after Melbourne;
there was only two arches and these nothing to the ones at
Melbourne, But I believe the reason was that they had their

ENTRANCE TO GOVERNMENT. HOUSE

day when they celebrated the Inauguration of the Commonwealth
the people also where very different and seemed more distant
and stuck up, in fact the only place that not only I, but,
all my chums took a fancy to, was the "Royal. Naval. House".
The Duke himself paid a visit to this place, and was so
pleased with it, that he personly complimented J. Shearston
the owner, and presented a large signed photo of himself

and the Duchess to the house; The people of Sydney seemed greatly impressed by the Russian Cruiser, and reckoned that she was a match for the remainder of the ships in the harbour, britishers included, put together. One evening was devoted by the ships of war, to illuminating, and as at "Melbourne", the foreigners knocked us out of time, but towards the later part of the evening, the Australian ships took the cake by making a water fall of fireworks, fall from their upper decks into the water, and it made a magnificent

H.M.S "BOOMERANG"

H.M.S. "KARAKATTA"

sight, and was prolonged for nearly an hour. The last two or three days of our stay, visitors where allowed on board and the Duke went shooting up country, It was on the morning of the 6th of June when their Royal Highnesses embarked and by twelve midday, we where slowly steaming down the harbour, with our escort in our wake bound for "New Zealand," The shores where much more crowded than when we came. in ten days before.

New Zealand.

MAORI IDOL

Auckland

We arrived at Devonport; a place quite close to "Auckland" on the 10th. Here we witnessed quite a unique incident; i.e. we perceived a small boat making for the ship, and as it got closer, we saw that a little girl was the sole occupant, she was a white girl, and no older than 10 yrs at the outside; she pulled beautifully, and came up along side in grand stile, although a nasty sea was running, One of the side boys went down the gangway to meet her, and she gave him a beautifull bouquet, and asked him to give it to the Duchess, needless to say it was accepted

The following morning the got up anchor and proceeded to Auckland, Over a dozen large passenger boats came out to meet us; and took up there positions astern, As we drew closer to our destination, we saw the shore was crowded with people, and they cheered themselves hourse, as we came up alongside the jetty. Their "Royal Highnesses" went ashore about 2 in the afternoon and met with a

AUCKLAND HARBOUR BOARD ARCH

great reception. An electric button was fitted upon the jetty so that "His Royal Highness" announced to the whole of Auckland his own landing. A splendid triumphal arch made of greenstuff, was erected at the head of the pier, and another at the other end representing two lighthouses. Joined by an arched span. Dense masses of people lined the route right to "Government House," and cheered again and again as their "Royal Highnesses", and escort, drove by. During our stay in Auckland the "Duke & Duchess" witnessed some Native dancing or as the Maories call it Haka, it is a kind of war dance, and without a doubt is the best style of savage dancing that one would find, if he searched the whole World over, To show what kind of people the "Maories" are, I relate the following; It appears that the evening before the Duke's visit, a great calamity fell on the natives, one of there greatest chiefs died Now this race bewails; loud and long; for days; at the death of any notable chief;

TAMATI WAKA NENE
A FAMOUS N.Z. CHIEF

but; this time, no one outside their own circle knew any thing about it, untill the Duke came and went, and then, and not till then, did the sounds of sorrow rise up into the air; The Duke also

KYWI

had some very good shooting, and bagged about 2 stags and 6 hinds." New Zealand" has some peculiar birds, and I give an illustration of the most peculiar. It was late in the evening of the 15th when their Royal Highnesses went ashore, and at daybreak the next morning we let go our hawsers, and turned our ships head for

Wellington, N.Z. When we got fairly out to sea, we found a heavy ground swell running, which made us pitch and roll a good deal; one of our escorts the Juno, took a different course to us, and we soon lost sight of her; the next day was spent at sea, and the weather was getting very miserable

HARBOUR BOARD ARCH

very cold, and a drizzling rain falling most of the time; in the evening we ran into "Wellington" harbour, it was about 7 p.m. and a dinner party was held on board, and the Govenor and others of note came off to the ship, We also found the same portion of the Australian squadron here that was at "Melbourne" Our trip from Auckland to Wellington was done in very good time nearly 600 miles in less than 48 hours

Wellington. N.Z.

The sort of weather we got at
Wellington

On the morning of the 18th June, admidst the thunder
of saluting guns; we made our way carefully along
side the jetty of "Breezy Wellington" as it is called
The weather was shocking, but cleared up a bit by
the time their Royal Highnesses landed, which
they did about 11 a.m; and as they drove through
the dock gates, they met with a most enthuastic
reception, and to make things better the sun made
several attempts to break through the heavy low
lying clouds, and made things livelier, Taking the
weather into consideration, their "Royal Highnesses"

had a remarkable drive through the city; the people thronged every available place along the whole line of route to Government House. The place to was most exceeding, well decorated, there being quite as many triumphal arches as there was at Melbourne, and one of them the (coal arch) beating all other arches we had yet seen. Altogether, taking into considering the sise of the place, there was an extraordinary show of

Bluejacket coaling ship

patriotic feeling. The day before leaving, a regetta was held in which the Navy played a prominent part. One thing I wish to mention is that this was the first place where the crew of the Ophir coaled ship, and we took in 800 tons, the above illustration shows the manner in which the bluejackets and marines, carried the coal, and you will understand it was exceedingly hard work when I say that each basket was about two cwt. During the regatta 3 submarine mines as they are commonly called where exploded one after the other, each blowing to atoms small representations of ships placed directly over each mine.

SUBMARINE EXPLOSION

NAVAL SUBMARINE MINE

On Friday June the 21st about half past 3 in the after noon Their "Royal Highnesses" embarked, and immediatly we cast of from the jetty; and despite the wretched weather the shore was crowded with people, who cheered again and again, as we swung our ships head for the mouth of the harbour; and together with our escort proceeded in our way to "Lyttelton" Two or three pleasure steamers accompanied us out of the harbour, but they soon found the sea to rough, and our speed to fast, and they turned back, It was quite dark by the time we got out to sea. The sea was pretty rough, and all along the coast at intervals huge beacons had been lit, and fairly lit up the coast line; we where off "Lyttelton" very early next morning, and as soon as it was daylight proceeded up the harbour, passing five ships of the Australian squadron who manned yards and saluted us, their ships companies cheering meantime We tied up alongside of a jetty, with a landing place all ready rigged up. with green stuff, and bunting. The Duke and Duchess and suite left the ship about 11 in the forenoon, and just before they stepped into the train that was to convey them to Christchurch, a large body of school children sang ("God Save the King") in good time, and good voice; the Duke and suite saluting meanwhile; They then stepped into the train admidst the cheers of the crowd, And then the train steamed slowly on its way to the beautifull city of "Christchurch"

The train had to pass through an exceedingly long tunnel, as Lyttelton is completely surrounded by mountains.

Lyttelton Canterbury
and
Christchurch

The weather here was bright and clear but very cold; and the train service free to the men of the visiting warships, so I made use of the opportunity and made a flying visit to "Christchurch," and

H.M.S. PYLADES   H.M.S. ARCHER   H.M.S. SPARROW   H.M.S. TORCH

found it a flourishing town, the decorations to were on a very lavish scale, and the arches very original, one being built of ice and frozen meat, and bearing the inscription (Frozen our product but warm our welcome) and another formed of livestock in cages including, cows, horse's, sheep, poultry, ect. The town also, was well illuminated as darkness set in.

The next day instead of going by train I climbed the high hills that lay between us and Christchurch and when I reached the top a glorious panarama presented itself to my gaze, a flat plain that at first looked like the sea, lay at my feet, but as I gazed I could just make out the tops of the

CHRISTCHURCH FROM THE HILLS

steeples and tall chimneys peeping through the mist ; whilst away in the far distance, was a range of noble mountains, It was a splendid sight and well worth the hard walk over the boulder strewn hills. I also visited a Maori village. but met with a dissapointment, I expected to find them in a semi civilised condition, but judge to my surprise

when I found them exactly the same as the Europeans
Same houses, same dress, same speach, in fact just the same as
English people, but for their brown skins, The sketch below
was taken up the river, some fifteen miles above Christ
church where as you can see, the scenery was most
bewitching, but
a hard frost setting
in, as soon as the
sun went down
made matters
a little bit
disagreeable, to
us, who only a short
time ago, where under
a scorching tropical sun

Sunrise in NewZealand

About midday on the 27th of June we slipped from the warf
and went out side, returning again in the evening, after
having adjusted our compasses, and dropped our anchor
in the gulf some distance from "Lyttelton," A heavy
swell was running and made us roll considerably.
It was about 8 pm, when we perceived the "Goveners

yacht approaching with the Royal Party on the saloon deck, she was brilliantly lit up with electricity, and as she came on rockets ascended in all directions. When she came loser we saw that there would be some difficulty in getting their "Royal Highnesses" from one ship to the other, the swell was so great, but after considerable trouble a gangboard was got out, and wating their first opportunity the Royal Party quickly ran on board the Duchess first, the Duke following; and only just in time; for the two ships came together with a crash and then rolled far apart, leaving the gang board dangling down from the Ophir's upper deck, One of our principal gangway ladders was smashed to matchwood also the lower boom, a long spar some fifteen or sixteen inches in diameter, A lot more damage was done but the Governers yacht suffered the most, she having some of her plates stove in and her bridge smashed, and after we got the "Royal Suite" and luggage on board, she left with all possible speed for "Lyttelton" to go in dock, and we got up anchor and proceeded on our way for "Tasmania; our escort

Wardroom & Crew

Provisioning Ship

"THE CREW'S SHARE"

THE WARDROOM'S SHARE

taking up their usual positions astern. The next morning was beautiful and clear, and the view shoreward was magnificent, the bright blue sea, and the light green hills, backed by hills of somber brown, behind which, towering into the purple sky was a range of noble snow capped mountains, making a grand picture. After passing through "Cooks Straits" we had a fair wind, and as we got further away from land the sea began to get rougher, and by midnight, the following day our good ship was rolling and tumbling about as bad, if not worse, than when we crossed the Bay, we shipped plenty of water and every place had a good share of it, I think the bakehouse suffered the most; I looked in and found the poor baker up to his waist in water loaves of bread, buns, dough, bags of flour, dishes baking tins ect. Several men where injured, and the Duchess must have been very ill; for as I have already mentioned, she was a victim to Mal-de-mere Most of the suite did not venture out of their cabins, but the "Duke" seemed quite at home;

a regular Sailor Prince, The ships company especially the seamen; where highly delighted with the turn of events; as to day was "Sunday," and they knew that there would be no divisions; a thing most + flat foots dread; as a most minute inspection is carried out then, On the mess deck they amused themselves by

GALE BETWEEN. N.Z. & TASMANIA

yelling like fiends; every time a sea came down the hatchway, and as this point of our journey was really the begining of our homeward passage. they sang their old favourite song ("Rolling home to Merry England") again and again, with great emphasis, The next day, the wind moderated a little; and the sea was much smoother We arrived at Hobart about 11 a.m. the 2nd of July.

+ Naval slang for "seaman."

Hobart
Tasmania

The following day we went alongside the pier, and I may state that they had prepared a much better landing stage, than we had previously met with in our tour. The people seemed exceedingly loyal; and the crisp bright wintry day, echoed and reechoed with hearty cheers; when their "Royal Highnesses" landed shortly after midday, The decorations also were very good, ferns like those in the illustration being largely used in the place of venetian masts; to line the streets, One of the principal events was the wood chopping contest, The champion wood chopper being present, I was not present myself but I heard Their Royal Highnesses were greatly impressed by the way huge trees were felled and cut up, in an incredibly short space of time What took my eye was "Mount Wellington" that formed the background of "Hobart", and as a lot of my shipmates said it would take a lot of climbing; In fact some said it would take a day to get up, I said I would go to the top plant a flag and be down the same day starting when we went ashore

The ascent of Mount Wellington.

I started about 1 p.m. and after buying a cheap flag which I meant to fix on the highest point, (The flag by the way was a French flag the only one available all the others having been sold) It was a walk of about six miles, To the foot of the mountain, I may here mention that a road led about two thirds of the way up, but as I never asked for information, I was ignorant of the fact until afterwards But anyhow I struck a timber track and started upwards in good spirits, but bad boots, These boots where the cause of much misery and hardship; in fact they where only a kind of leather slipper, served out to the seamen of the "Ophir," so as not to make a noise, when running about the ship, on the days we where supposed to wear boots, Sundays ect And the sailors gave them the glorified name of the "Royal Pumps." Well after following the timber track for about a mile; passing many fallen monarchs of the forrest, it ended in a couple of small paths, hardly traceable in places, I followed the one I thought best and soon found myself in the thick of the forrest. The scenery was grand, nearly all the trees, were stripped of their bark, and stood up like columns of light against the dark background, on some of the trees the bark hung in long festunes from the branches

IN THE FOREST.

a hundred feet from the ground, and the gentle breeze swung it backwards and forward, like an immense pendulum., making a peculiar rattling sound, as it touched the neighbouring tree trunks. The under groath now began to get so thick it was well nigh impassable, and I noticed that a large number of the fallen trees had been brought down by fire; but no trace of fire could be seen in the underwood. It was astonishing how the fire had hardened the burnt trees. In some places the remnants of a tree stood up several feet burnt out to a fine point as hard and sharp as a needle. The ground began to change, it rar up much steeper, the trees smaller, and in place of the tangled underwood, were rocks; all sizes, intermingled with a long dry tough grass, that came in very handy in hauling ones self from rock to rock, I now paused to take a breath, and look round. I could not see the top of the mountain, it was enveloped in clouds, but I had a splendid view of the town, the harbour, and the shipping. But I had no time to loose if I was going to reach the summit, which I had told my shipmates I intended doing. So I once more started upwards, it was now about 5 p.m. as near as I could guess; as I had no watch, and felt like sitting down to a good tea, I now began to find snow in between the rocks, and I began to get so thirsty that from time. I quenched it with pieces of frozen snow. The rocks now got bigger and bigger, and the side of the mountain steeper; and now and then the clouds would drift by and expose the mountain top to view, but it seemed a long way off yet; but I still struggled on the snow getting deeper the crust of which was frozen hard, and would bear ones weight—

IN. THE SNOW LINE

but now and then it would give way and I found myself in different depths up to ten or twelve feet. but I managed to extract myself each time from these awkward positions. My feet now began to get in a shocking state, the snow turned my "Royal pumps" into raw hide again, and made it a very slippery job climbing from rock to rock. The patches of snow where now 20 or 30 ft in extent, and I crossed these on my hands and knees, not knowing to what depth I may desend, if the hard crust gave way, I now came to a wall of rock sixty feet high, and as I saw no other way of getting up proceeded to climb it inch by inch, foot by foot until I reached the top. Snow was now falling in sheets, winding about in all directions, and I waited till it lifted a little, when I saw what appeared to be the summit a few hundred feet in front and above me. I now began to feel the cold, but I pushed on as it was rapidly getting dark, and passing an half dead tree broke off a branch about 15 feet in length to act

HAULING UP
THE FLAG
STAFF

as a flag staff. When I reached what I thought was the top the view was rather clear, and I perceived the rocks ran up much higher yet, but I struggled on determined not to give in, After climbing another pile of rocks, I was enveloped in another snow cloud, as cold as ice; and the wind blew half a gale, the snow drifting by in heaps, all was black now except the snow, I found

THE SUMMIT

shelter between two large rocks, and waited for it to blow over I felt like lying down and going to sleep, but having read in books, it is fatal to do so in such cases, fought hard against the feeling. But the snow blast went as quickly as it came, and the moon shone out cold and clear. So I clambered on the largest rock and saw to my great joy that at last I was on the top, at last I had arrived at the topmost peak; so I quickly bound flag to the branch, and jammed it down between two rocks. It was as much as I could do, the cold was so intense, so I started to desend as quickly as possible, but not the same way as I came up, I soon came to a bit of a gully, the snow sloping away into the darkness beneath, I meant to cross this, but in doing so, started to slide downwards, so I turned on my back, and dug my heels deep into the snow, this checked me, but then the idea struck me, to slide down the mountain side, I was getting desperate, and would do anything to get out of the icy atmosphere. So away I slid into the darkness. I was thankfull afterwards dhat I did not go over a precipice; but I did not care at the time, for was I not getting to warmer air, away from the rocks, frost, and snow. I think I must have desended, several hundred feet like this when I found the bushes and rocks getting too thick to tobaggan any farther; so I started to clamber over the rocks once more; letting myself down by the grass and bushes. The moon was now shining brightly and after toiling for an hour or more, over rougher ground than any previously met with; I began to feel warmer; the thick bush, and tangled masses of vegetation again putting in an appearance, and the farther I desended into the forrest the darker it became; untill I could not see an arm's length in front of me; for the trees were so high that the moon failed to penetrate; and so I toiled on through the thick bushes, barking my shins against fallen timber falling over tree trunks, with only one, or at least a part of one shoe on, the other having dissapeared long ago; now and then a branch knocked my cap off, and I had difficulty in finding it again even with the aid of matches, which I luckily possessed, as I desended the ground got moister and in some places I went in up to my knees, a kind of stinging nettle also gave me a lot of inconvenience, and from time to time a thorn entered my feet, even penetrating the odd shoe; and I thought what a fool I was to venture on such a trip alone and at such a time, But I had the consolation that I had accomplished my task, and it was close on midnight when I stumbled across a road, yes a regular smooth flat road, and I was as happy as a king, After walking some distance, I came to an hotel, and as they had not retired I was able to get refreshments; and they seemed immencly surprised when I said I had just come from the mountain top and all alone, I left there about half past twelve and after walking another six miles, arrived on board more dead than alive, The next morning with the aid of a powerfull glass the flag could be seen from the ship, but I had to go to bed with bad feet and aching limbs

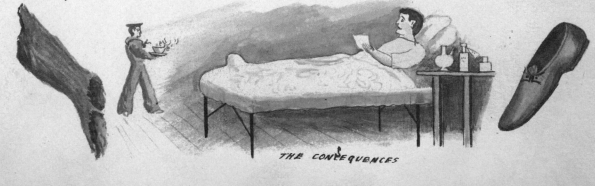

THE CONSEQUENCES

I dont know much about the next few days, that is of the outside world as I was hors - de - combat. but their "Royal Highnesses" had a good send when we left on the sixth; by the amount of noise and cheering outside. The next time I came on deck, I found we where anchored off the mouth of the river leading up to "Port Adelaide", Their "Royal Highnesses" left the ship the following day, and next morning we went up the river, and tied up alongside jetty.

Adelaide.
South Australia.

Going up the river to Adelaide greatly resembles the Suez Canal; the river being very narrow, and the land lying very low, stretching away for miles. A very pretty landing stage was erected on the jetty, made of evergreens and sheaves of corn and wheat relieved, with coats of

arms etc, I believe their "Royal Highnesses" had a grand time ashore; I am sure the "Ophir's" ships company did. Our band gave three concerts in the "Town Hall," which were well attended Our theatrical troup also gave a concert which was much appreciated; although the attendance was not great; owing to greater counter attractions. The following friday was visitors day, and I can safely say we had more people on board. than we have, had, on any previous occasion; It is quite enough; when I say that quite a number of ladies fainted, and the bluejackets and marines had their hands full. But I think the principal feature of their "Royal Highnesses" stay in Adelaide, was the most enthusiastic send off they had when leaving It was early in the morning of the 15th of July;

when the people began to assemble round and about the jetty where the "Ophir" lay; by mid day dense masses of people had arrived; and with them came about 300 little boys and girls dressed in sailors clothes, the boys carrying a small wooden cutlass, and the girls small "Union Jacks," a "Guard of Honour" was also drawn up on the platform leading from the train to the ship. About one o'clock the train

One of the Ophirs pets a Laughing Jackass

H.M. Colonial. Ship. "Protector."

conveying their "Royal Highnesses" arrived and was heralded by the cheers of the multitude; As soon as the "Royal Party" had alighted; and shaken hands, and wished good byeto their large number of friends; They proceeded on board, The "Duke" hardly looking so well as usual; but the Duchess looked radiant with heath and beauty. The suite also looked in good health and sprits About 2 p.m we proceeded to cast off from the Jetty and a couple of Tugs hauled us off, As soon as we began to move; the cheers were deffening and above all could be heard the boys and girls before mentioned; They even stood on their toes in giving full force to their lungs, With their wooden swords and flags waving frantically in the air, Our band now began to play "Auld

Lang—Syne", and a hush fell on the crowd;
"the "Royal Party" on the promenade deck drinking
their health meanwhile; I saw several women and
men with tears in their eyes as the old familiar
tune was heard; one old lady was crying out right,
and many a heart must have gone thousands of
miles across the sea; to the dear old "Home land".
The instant the band finished, a cheer went up
simultainiously, and must have been heard for miles.
The band now played "Rule Britannia" and we proceed
ed down the river; escorted by H.M.C.S. Protector.
When we got to the mouth of the river; we found
the Royal Arthur awaiting to escort us to
Freemantle

In the
great Australian
Bight
——
Sunset
~~~

H.M.S. "Royal Arthur."

Our passage across the great "Australian Bight" was rather stormy, and gradually increased in vlence; in the next few days, especially; when

Wild life in
Australia
—
The Cassowary

we altered course, and turned up the west coast. On the friday we where close to "Freemantle"

THE "S.S. BRITANNIC" WITH AUSTRALIAN TROOPS HOMEWARD BOUND FROM "SOUTH AFRICA." ENTERING ALBANY.

but the weather was now so bad that it was thought adviseable to turn back, and run into Albany; which we did and arrived there about 2-a.m. on Sunday; and about 7-a.m. went right up the harbour, and made fast to the railway jetty! Our arrival causing no small stir amongst the few people left in the town; as most of them had gone up to "Freemantle" by train. In the afternoon we sighted a large white steamer off the mouth of the harbour, which turned out to be the "SS Britannic" with "Australian Bushmen" homeward bound from "S. Africa". This was the seccond time we met with this beautiful ship carrying troops. When we perceived that she was coming up the harbour; we turned up the band and all hands, as also did the "Royal Arthur". I forgot to mention that our two watchdogs where

here the "St George and Juno," Well as the "Britannic"
passed between us and the "Royal Arthur" our crew
gave three rousing cheers; repeated on the "Britannic"
by the Bushmen, who went nearly mad when they
recognised the "Duke and Duchess," The "Arthurs" now
began to cheer, followed by the "Juno's" and our
band where doing their level best, playing "Soldiers
of the Queen," and then "Rule Britannia" etc, I dont
think the harbour of Albany had ever seen or
heard the likes before, the troopship anchored
close to us, numbers of the troops remaining up
the rigging for some time, The next morning
the "Royal Party" left the ship and proceeded
by train to "Freemantle," and we proceeded
to take in 450 tons of coal, and we had finished
and was under weigh by seven in the morning
bound for "Freemantle" arriving there in
very fine weather the 23rd of July.

Western Australia

Freemantle
&
Perth

Most of our time here was spent in
getting 1450 tons of coal into our bunkers
after which I managed to run up to "Perth"
for a few hours, and it a flourishing city
well decorated and the arches where some
of the best we had yet seen, and the people
just as loyal and enthuastic as ever, but the
great event was. "The farewell to Australia"
Like "Adelaide" the people began to assemble early
in the morning; but in much larger numbers
by eleven in the forenoon a dense mass of people
had monopolised every inch of space on the

THE GOLD ARCH AT PERTH. THE GILDED PORTIONS REPRESENTED THE TOTAL AMOUNT, IN CUBIC INCHES OF GOLD, TAKEN OUT, SINCE ITS DISCOVERY

wharf, Opposite the ship a large gallery had been erected, this was packed with ticket holders and at one end of it was two or three thousand school children each with a "National flag". The arrival of the "Duke and Duchess" was first heralded by the thunder of the "Royal Arthurs" guns, saluting. The "Royal Party" landed by entering the "Ophir" the starboard side, and then walking across the ship and out the opposite side, on to the wharf; their appearance being the signal for a tremendous outburst of cheering on the part of the multitude; the "Duke and Duchess" acknowledging it by bowing to the right and left; After shaking hands etc, with all the big men of the town, they walked up to where the children sat; As their "Royal Highnesses" approached, they burst into a shrill cheer waving their flags franticly, but after no little difficulty the teachers restored order, and as the band played the "King", the children burst forth into song, singing the first two verses of the "National Anthem", and then began to cheer and wave their flags; again their childish voices rising high above the hoarser and deeper cheers of the crowd; It was an impressive sight and one not easily forgotten. The "Duke and Duchess" now walked back to where a canopy had been erected over the head of the first pile; A model of a pile driver, with a bottle of champagne for the driver, was also rigged up. The "Duchess" was now asked to step up on the platform and christen the pier, first an address was red out explaining all about the pier, the amount of wood, ect, the "President" of the committe now gave the "Duchess" a pair of scissors, with which she cut the cord suspending the bottle; at the same time naming the pier "Victoria" The bottle fell and smashed on the head of the pile, whilst the cheers of the people broke out afresh; Their "Royal Highnesses" now walked back to where all the notables where gathered, and one by one they wished them all good by, shaking hands with each one individually; and as their "Royal Highnesses" turned to proceed on board, the cheering

was deffening

Farewell
to
Australasia

26ᵗʰ July.01.

A farewell luncheon was held on board
between the hours of one and two, after which
all guests left the ship, "Lady Lawley" had
tears in her eyes, as her little son remained
on board, to take passage to "England," The
sailors where now very busy casting off
the large steel hawsers, which secured the
"Ophir" to the pier. As soon as the tugs started
to haul us away from shore, the pent up
feelings of the people ashore, could not be

restrained longer, and a tremendous cheer went upwards, whilst the bands played The "King", Our band now began to play "For-auld-lang-syne", which set all the people singing, At the conclusion the cheering was louder than ever; "Rule Britannia"

THE ROYAL ARTHUR'S FAREWELL

came next. and then "Home sweet Home", The huge crowds became very quiet as this was played; except for one man who stood on his head. We now began to move slowly down the harbour, their "Royal Highnesses" on the bridge, The Duke now turned to the crew of the "Ophir" and cried; three cheers for

"Australia," which we gave right heartily, and set the hundreds of thousands ashore. Cheering again. As we passed slowly down the harbour by steamers and sailing ships, each one a mass of human beings, the noise was deffening, hooters whistles, bells, each vied with one another in making the most noise; but as we increased our speed, we soon left everything far astern, and the "Royal Arthur," came up astern to act as escort In a few hours "Australia" was a thin grey line astern; gradually getting more indistinct until it dissapeared altogether, yes the land where we had spent many an happy hour was gone. but not forgotten. That night the "Royal Arthur" wished us fare well, by firing rockets and displaying on her side the word farewell in electric lights, and she made a very pretty picture indeed. In the middle watch searchlights flashed on the sky line miles ahead, which afterwards turned out to be the "Juno" signaling

Our next place of call was "Mauritius," the journey occupied nine days in which some interesting events took place. In the first place some sports took place and prizes, such as watches, knives, pencil cases, clocks, etc, where given by the "Duke & Duchess" it went off very well indeed; and Their "Royal Highnesses" were exceedingly amused at the capers of the men, as the ship was rolling and pitching somewhat

THE
WHEELBARROW
RACE
-
SHIPS SPORTS

The Tug of war and most of the other events were won by the bluejackets, The next day the whole of the crew of the "Ophir" mustered on the boat deck, which had been made a bit ship shape; The Duke and Duchess, with their Suite,

Then arrived and took their positions in the center of the group; and the ships photographer took about four or five negetaves; and then we all dispersed. It pleases me here to state that the "Duke" said he would like to see this log book and I at once complied with his request, and when it was returned, they sent word that they where delighted with it, and would like to see it again at a later date, We sighted the "St George" the next day, and the following sunday afternoon; about four o'clock we ran into "Mauritius", and dropped both anchors making our stern fast to a buoy.

Mauritius

Here we found an old friend "H.M.S. Highflier." and with her "H.M.S. Cossack." Their "Royal Highnesses" and Suite, went ashore the next day; but I know nothing of what happened on shore as non of the crew were allowed leave; because of the plague. Like "Freemantle" our time here was nearly all occupied coaling ship, We had about 250 men to assist us, from the "Highflier" and "Cossack," and then it took us considerably more than twenty four hours to take in one thousand one hundred tons, these men where victualed on board of us; and seemed surprised when they got sausages and mash for breakfast. On the 8th of August, their "Royal Highnesses" returned to the ship. and after luncheon, we got up anchors. and after all guests had gone over the side, we swung round, and admidst the cheers of the "Highflier; Cossack," and the soldiers on shore, we slowly steamed away, increasing our

speed, untill our usuall forteen knots was
reached, with our escort in their usual positions
"Durban" was our next port of call, and as the
weather was exceedingly fine we expected to
make a good run of it. But our expectations
where doomed to be disappointed, as it soon
got rough, and the "St George" made a very

THE
ST GEORGE
MAKING A BAD PASSAGE

bad passage of it, pitching to an alarming
extent and taking tons of water on her
fo-castle, which ran off again, as she rose
on the next sea, pouring down her sides
like a waterfall. On the evening of the 12th Aug
a memorable service was held in the grand

saloon, in memoriam of the late "Empress Frederick Dowager", The next day we sighted the coast of "Natal" and soon afterwards where anchored off the town of "Durban"

South Africa

Durban

The "Ophir" was too big a ship to cross the bar, so instead of going right inside the harbour we had to content ourselves with staying outside, which was nearly as bad as being at sea, the rollers, rushing in from seaward making it a risky job, in embarking on the splendid tugs, with which the port is well supplied. "Their Royal Highnesses" with part of their suite, left the ship with safety about 11 a,m, on the 19th inst.

One way of transfering passengers from ships to the tug boats is to hoist them out like merchandise; in large baskets; This method was only used by us once when "Lady Catherine Coke," The Duke of Roxburg & Mr & Mrs Dereck Keppel came back to the ship. Several large sharks were observed around the ship here. Part of the Cape squadron was here also to take part in the ceremonies; the S^{n}

"George & Juno" having go on to "Cape Town." The

ships here were the "Gibralta" flagship the

"Thrush & Dwarfe" gunboats, and the "Barracouta"

third class cruiser. "Their Royal Highnesses"

returned to the ship, on the 15th Aug and we

immediatly got under weigh and escorted

H.M.S. THRUSH.   H.M.S. GIBRALTAR.

by the "Gibralta" turned our ships head for

"Cape Town," When leaving two large black

fish; a species of whale crossed our bows

a few feet away and then commenced

to blow, I should put them down as being

between 30 and 40 feet in length. We had very bad weather as soon as we were well out at sea; which delayed us considerably, so that we arrived at Simons Town on Sunday 18th Aug. instead of the preceeding day

Simonstown & Capetown

H.M.S. Partridge.

Simons Bay.

As we proceeded up the bay, we saw on our left hand a Boer prisoners camp, it was early morn and but few Boer's were astir, but the ever watchfull sentries could be plainly seen and as they turned on their beat, something shone forth like burnished silver over each mans shoulder

H.M.S. FORTE.

H.M.S. MONARCH

H.M.S. NAIAD

H.M.S. TERPICHORE

It was the sun shining on the blades of fixed bayonets. In Simons bay we found the following British men-of-war; the "Monarch, Forte, Partridge, Terpischore, Naide," and the prison ship "Penelope," together with our old escort. the "St George and Juno" We occupied the "Monarch's" moorings, Their Royal Highnesses" did not land till monday; As they where pulled ashore all the ships saluted, The noise of the guns echoing and re echoing amongst the lofty hills, which surround

PRISON SHIP

the town; As Their Royal Highnesses" landed an interesting affair was, that they where drawn in their carriage by bluejackets, instead of horses, all the way to the station. The

"Duke & Duchess", with their suite at once entrained and proceeded to "Capetown", The "St. George" and "Juno," also weighed anchor, and left for "Capetown," but we immediately prepared for coaling, and by mid day we, together with some three hundred men from the "Gibraltar Forte Partridge Monarch Naïade Terpsichore", and some

seedy boys or blacks, where up to our eyes in coal dust, We finished coaling about midnight on Tuesday having got in about

twelve hundred tons, the following day we had our hands full cleaning ship, but we got over it all right, and in the evening all the warships gave us a fine display of fireworks

I may here mention that on this day a large number of native chiefs, sent by "His Royal Highness, the Duke," went on board the "Monarch", and there witnessed the firing of the big guns, outrigger charges, submarine mines etc; and they went away, I reckon, more impressed than ever, with the great nation, under whose protection they lived. About midday the following day the 22nd Aug their "Royal Highnesses," embarked, and we at once slipped our moorings, and with the "Naiade and Terpeschore" as escort; we proceeded on our way; the "St George and Juno." had previously received orders to go on to "St Helena." The "Partridge" also came with us, "Admiral Moore" being on board of her. We shaped our course past "Capetown" and in the distance could just make out Table Mountain. The

"Partridge" now turned back, and we increased speed, the high land of the "Cape" rapidly getting lower and more indistinct. But in leaving "South Africa" none of the feelings like we experienced when leaving "Australia" affected us, we had seen so very little of the shore

The last of South Africa

Nothing of any importance took place until the evening of the 26th., when the ship nigger troop gave a concert, and it passed off very well indeed, I may here mention that several entertainment had been given since I mentioned the last one. For some two or

Three months back, the officers had been practicing for a "Nautical Burlesque", and "Chevalier-de-Martino" was painting some scenery for it. About 4·a·m, on the 28ᵗʰ inst.

The "Ophir" ⋯⋯ Minstrel Troupe

Bones	Interloactor	Tambo
P.O.II J. Howe	Gr. T. Wright	P.O.I R. Stone.

Accompanist --- F. Daniels RMLI.

PROGRAMME

Overture	– – –	Tambo Bones & Piano.
Opening Chorus	"Ring Tailed Coon"	Troupe.
Song of the Toreador	(From Carmen)	Gnr. J. Cowling.
Comic Song	"I'd like to go halves in that"	P.O.II J. Howe.
Coon Song	"Lily of Laguna"	P.O.II H. Price
Song	"Take a little Patsy"	Gnr - T. Wright
Song	"The Lost Chord"	Sgt. S. Dacombe
Song and Dance	"Song of Ireland"	Ldg. Sea. A. Silvie
Comic Song	"County Ball at Sligo"	Pte. W. Hickson
Song	"Johns Bull's Letter Bag"	Bugler. H. Kiddle
Song	"The Coons Courtship"	P.O.I R Stone
Final Chorus	"Dixie's Land"	Troupe

GOD SAVE THE KING

August 26ᵗʰ 1901

we passed "Sᵗ Helena," here we where met with the "Sᵗ George and Juno," who took over their old duty, whilst the "Terpsichore" and "Naiad," left us to carry out their work all up and down the east and west coast of Africa. I may here mention that on board, was a large number of pets. etc, at every turn one was confronted by cages containing parrots and paroquets of every shade colour and discription. Also cockatoo's in large numbers, besides quite

a host of smaller birds, We also had a pair of laughing jackasses and a sort of white kywi. In the animal line was a fawn &

SHIPS PETS

a few oppossum's, including a large white one; We also had a case of large lizards but these all died; From time to time in This book I give illustrations of some of them; None of the crew was allowed to have any live stock in the ship; or else the "Ophir" would have been turned into a floating menagery. We also had a mail for the "St George and Juno" and on the morning of the 29th we hove to., and they lowered their sea boats, came alongside of us; received

DIAMOND SPARROW

their mail and went back to their respective ships, whilst we did not wait, but went

full speed ahead, and it took out escort
a few hours to catch us up again. It was
now getting very warm. Once again we
were entering the
"Tropical Zone;"
Dolphins; also
shoales of flying
fish, again put
in an appearence;
but they were

PET FAWN.

of a much larger kind than those we saw

FLYING FISH.

In the Indian Ocean, and thereabouts; during our voyage out to Australia. On the evening of the 29th; the much talked of Nautical Burlesque came off and was

"A TRAGEDY."
(IN TWO ACTS.)

Who has not read all the details of the shocking outbreak on board H.M.S. "Mantelpiece."

By great good fortune the services of the original actors have been secured, and they are all tamed now, and does it not speak volumes for the system of Naval Discipline, not one of them is dangerous.

Are not their names in history?—so why trouble you with useless recapitulation.

It is entirely due to Mr Wright that the natural tension is somewhat eased by a little music—lest the grim story of the outbreak should cause a breakdown amongst the spectators.

The quarter deck of H.M.S. Mantelpiece has been secured! Can realism be realised more realistically.

GOD SAVE THE KING.

AUGUST. 29th 1901

a complete success; well worth the months of work and practice. The dresses where very good indeed; in fact the whole concern, scenery

effects etc, were excellent, Especially when I say

that all of it was made out of material that

was available on board, Below I give some

thing of what the stage was like, also the

principal parts of the play; where petty officer

"William Lee" shoots Captain

The play itself, is about a commander who

lets his crew do what they like, he is put

on half pay; and is substituted by a captain who

makes things hum in general; and causes a

mutiny, in which the crew draw lots to shoot the tyrannical skipper, it falls to the lot of the late commander's coxwain, to do the deed; this he successfully accomplishes, and to the crew,s great joy, their late captain is again put in command. During the jolly fications, at his return, the supposed dead body of the murdered captain comes to life, and he forgives and is forgiven. Tropical showers now began to get very frequent, and our friend, "Ventilation," again put in an appearance On sunday 1st sept, in the afternoon, we had a downfall of rain, lasting for two or three hours, it fell so thickly, that our escorts where invisable, though they were steaming pretty close to us. After it was over the sea became very smooth, this was the first smooth sea we have had for some months, and we were enabled now to open our ports on the mess deck, I may mention that only in very calm weather is it possible to do this, or else we should have our messes washed out; but now we were enabled to get a little fresh air

SEAMEN IN TROPICAL & SUB-TROPICAL CLOTHING

and we wanted it I assure you, for our place was like an oven, I give an illustration above, of the sort of clothing wore in the Tropics, of course every one knows that sailors have different clothes for the different climes, but few know the different kinds of rig, at least what they look like. From time to time if time permits I will give the different dresses of the British seaman. We arrived off S.t Vincent on the evening of the third of September & there found two warships illuminated which turned out to be our first escort the "Niobe and Diadem", that escorted us from. Portsmouth to Gibraltar. We dropped our anchor right midway between these two ships; and the same evening "H.M.S Mantelpiece" was again enacted, as a farewell concert for the "S.t George and Juno", as their place was to be taken by the more powerfull ships the "Niobe and Diadem". The officers of these ships were also present at the

Diferent Races of People met with During the Tour.

MALTESE LADY

ARAB

MALAY

AUSTRALIAN ABORIGINAL

WEST AFRICAN

AMERICAN INDIAN

entertainment, the officers of the afforesaid ships, were delighted with it, and were more so afterwards down in the wardroom, the sounds of revelry continuing far into the night. Below I give an appropriate piece of poetry recited during the performance
by
Prince. Alexandria
of Teck

Farewell to the "St George and Juno"

Oh mariniers of England,- and those who live at ease,
Remember those two cruisers; which ploughed through many seas.
Steady on either quarter - to guard the White York Rose
To stand twixt it and danger-wher-eir the "Ophir" goes
——— "' ———

Twas coaling here, and coaling there, twas coal at every port,
Twas quarantine for weeke and weeks, provisions running short.
And not till St Helena - did they there harvest reap
The first feed since Port Adelaide - a fine fat frozen sheep
——— "" ———

Our sympathies are all with those
Whose escort duties now must close

H. M. S. "JUNO"

St. Vincent.

NAPOLEON'S HILL

Our stay here, as at most of the ports
of call lately, was wholey taken up
coaling ship, We had the assistance
of a large number of bluejackets from
The "Niobe and Juno," a good few from
the first named ship turned out to
be old friends. from "H.M.S. Britannia."
the ship I left when I joined the Ophir,
so I was all right, and so were they, Their
"Royal Highnesses," stayed on board the
"St George" during the day time returning
at night to the "Ophir" to sleep, etc

On the evening following the one we came in, a large troopship crowded with troops came in, and left again about 4 pm the next day. We finished coaling about the same time as she left, and we at once prepared for for sea, and got everything ready for weighing anchor immediatly Their "Royal —

BIRD ISLAND

Highnesses" now returned to the ship and about.6.pm we weighed anchor and proceeded slowly out of harbour passing

PORTUGUESE GUNBOAT

close to the "St George and Juno," and
they manned the ship, and rigging, and
gave us three cheers, whilst our band
played "Auld-lang-syne," we passed quite
close to bird island, an allmost inaccessible
rock with a light house perched on top. A
Portuguese, gunboat accompanied us out
of harbour with manned yards, also our
new escort, two ships, that were splendid
specimens of "Britain's Naval. Might," each
one over 12,000 tons displacement, and
close on 500 feet in length, with a
speed of 22 knots. As we increased
our speed the little "Portuguese"
gunboat was soon left far astern,
when we got fairly out to sea, we
found it like a sheet of glass, and

up an application and information sheet at the Main L
or West End Library. Fill out the application, get pare
the Reference Desk at the Main Library. There will be
abilities and to set up teams of coaches who complen
who need help.

The application deadline is Wednesday, Septembe
After you submit your application we will contact you w

Interviews will be held beginning the week of Septemb

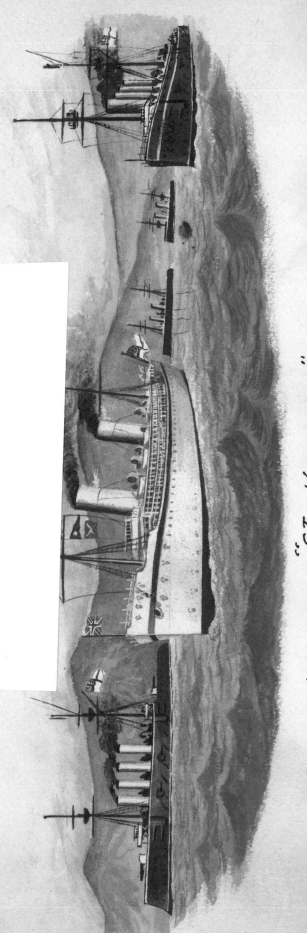

LEAVING "S! VINCENT."

when night fell it was delightfull;
a cool breeze just put a faint ripple
on the water, and made the air cool
and refreshing; after the heat of the
day, For the weather was quite hot
yet; though we had crossed the line
some considerable time. The next day
the sea was like a sheet of glass, but in
the middle watch the following night,
it began to blow hard, and by daylight
the next day, the sea was, as the saying goes,
mountains high, It soon got so bad that
we had to ease down, It lasted for three
days, and then moderated enough, that
we were able to go ahead again, full speed.
But one thing I could not make out was
although we where steering a northerly

course, the weather still remained the same; I mean as regards the heat; this may seem surprising when I say that we were steaming over three hundred miles each day, Masses

MORE PETS

of seaweed floated past our ship; for we were in the "Gulf Stream," and a large number of my ship mates, said that this gigantic current was the cause of the warm weather following us, We were now well in the track of ships, and were continually.

H.M.S. "OPHIR."

SEA ROUTINE

A.M.

4.0	Call the watch
4.10	Watch to muster, scrub and wash clothes, except Sundays.
5.30	Daymen lash up and stow hammocks, watch fall in, clean boat deck.
6.0	Marines and daymen fall in.
6.10	Part of ship of watch lash up and stow, cooks, stand easy.
6.45	Out pipes, Hands fall in, scrub after part of upper deck.
7.30	Sound the charge.
7.45	Sound off cooks.
8.0	Breakfast, hands to wash.
8.35	Up all wet towels on the towel lines.
8.40	Out pipes, watch below clean mess deck, watch clean fore part of upper deck
9.25	Hands to clean, down all towels.
9.40	Stow bags
9.45	Cooks watch below clear up mess deck remainder of both watches clear up the upper deck.
9.55	Sound the G.
10.0	Divisions, etc.
NOON	Sound the charge.

P.M

12.15	Sound off cooks.
12.30	Dinner,
1.50	Out pipes clear up decks.
2.0	Watch fall in, tell off for work.
4.15	Out pipes watch fall in clear up decks.
4.30	Divisions,
7.15	Marines stand by hammocks.
7.30	Seamen stand by hammocks.
8.0	Clear up decks.
9.0	Rounds.
10.0	Pipe down.

"INTERJECTION"

It will be noticed by the reader, that very little is mentioned, about the movements of their "Royal Highnesses", when ashore, at the different ports of call.

This is because the writer for several reasons did not know himself.

Although we on board the "Ophir" were interested in the doings of their "Royal Highnesses"; we had other things to attend to, for, at most places, when the "Duke & Duchess" were attending functions ashore; we were busy, coaling, or cleaning ship, or carring out work, which as members of the crew, it was our duty to do; So all I ask, is, that the reader of this log, should look on this narative as just the expression of a lower deck, seaman on what is an "historic event."

Also the author would like to point out that the book was written & illustrated during the voyage.

passing them, One sailing ship had a narrow escape of being run down by the "Niobe," in the darkness of the night. On the 12th; in the afternoon, there should have been deck sports, but at the last minute, dirty weather again set in, and it had to be postponed All the crew were now well used to the routine, though somewhat different to a man-of-war's, and things were running pretty smoothly. I give the routine on the preceeding page, just as it is posted up in the ship. But there was one thing I dont think we should ever get used to and that was "Old Ventilation", as it was called. Perhaps you dont understand but I will try and explain. On the boat or uppermost deck, where hundreds of cowls or venterlators as they are called, and sashlights

Now, as long as the weather is fine; venterlators

are trimed to the breeze, and the sashes open;

and all goes well; but at the approach of

rain, the well known cry of the boswains

mate is heard ("Watch close ventilation") and

then the fun starts, all the cowls must be

turned away from the wind, and the sashes

closed down, and they are so numerous

A SMALL
SECTION OF THE
"OPHIRS"
VENTILATON

that one is almost certain to get wet

through, And very often the rain has

passed, and it is fine again, before the
ventilation is all closed, it was a scource
of continual worry; and this trip we
were having a full dose of it, night and
day. One more thing I may mention was
"Physic's or Physical drill," of which we
got plenty, and our commander was a

PHYSICAL
DRILL

"KNEES"
UP

regular school of physical culture, and
never seemed so happy, as when he had
charge during the drill, Especially when
he ordered "knees up," (see Illustration).
To day a large number of stormy petrels
put in an appearance, I think this was

the first time during the voyage that we
have met with these interesting little birds.
They did not come close enough to the ship for
me to take a sketch of them. In the middle watch
the following night a fog
came on, Our commodore
instantly signaled to
take up formation single
line ahead, that is I mean
to our escort, And we got
out fog-bouys, you will
see what I mean, They
are towed astern, and

FOG-BOUYS

the next ship can tell when they are close
upon you, (see illustration) With the fog
came colder weather. On the following
afternoon, we had our deck sports, and
although the entries, were far short of

when we held deck sports, between "Fre
mantle and Mauritius," they went of
just as well, and better prizes were presented
by the "Duke," One of the prize's very much
appreciated was a pipe, with the "Duke of Cornwall
and York's" crest engraved on the silver mount

DECK SPORTS
THE OBSTACLE RACE

Just as the sports were drawing to a finish
a man-of-war was sighted of our port bow
and she turned out to be "H.M.S. Indefatigable"
of the "North America and West Indies —
Squadron," with mails for us. We hove too,
and she lowered a boat, and brought

our mails; together with a pilot to navigate
us up the "St Lawrence". The "Niobe and Diadem"
also sent their sea boats for mails, As soon
as this little transaction was over, she went

PICKING U
MAILS AT SEA

of in a southerly direction; presumably
to "Halifax N.S." By sunset we were entering
the gulf of "St Lawrence". About two hours
afterwards, a dence fog came on, and we
we again repeated the manouvers of the
following night; fog-bouys etc, whilst we
also used our fog-horn frequently; and

and so did our escort; who were now joined by "H.M.S. Tribune," cruiser, sister ship to the "Indefatigable," Extra look outs were also posted on the fo-castle; and water tight doors closed; In fact every thing that could be done, to ensure the safety of the "Ophir". But by two O.clock the following day the fog had lifted again, so we increased our speed once more. At day break we found a Torpedo boat destroyer off our

"H.M.S." "QUAIL".

port quarter, which tured out to be "H.M.S Quail." We had quite an exciting

incident with this little craft later on
in the forenoon; it was about half past nine.
We had despatches for her; and instead of
stopping to give them to her, we rigged out
the lower boom, and made the papers fast to
a rope rove through
a block at the end
of it, for all the
world like a
fishing line. We
were steaming about
fifteen knots at (AN EXCITING MOMENT)
the time, but she came up alongside quite
easily, but a little to far out to reach the
bag; she then made another try, and wether
we moved our helm or not I cant say; but just

as they reached the papers, the destroyer was drawn right under our bows, and as we came together, she heeled over alarmingly; and the ashes came up her funnels in dense clouds, But as you know these boats have an extraordinary speed, so she went full speed ahead, and just managed to slip round the other side of us, missing our stem by a few inches only, Every one was much relieved, when she got clear; as it was a wonder, something more serious did not happen. We were now entering well into the river; but little could be seen, except an occasional glimse of the shore, here and there, as the fog lifted. We were now wearing No 3.

dress, (serge suits) because of the cold, and the next day we put on extra clothing in the shape of Jersey's. On saturday night in the middle watch, we dropped anchor, but as soon as it was daylight, we got under

LANDING RIG . WINTER
Nº 3ᵈ JERSEYS CUTLASS AND PISTOL

weigh again. We then steamed slowly untill about two O-clock Sunday afternoon; when the fog again enveloped us, and we again anchored, and shortly afterwards got under weigh again, It was getting rather monotonous, we knew that we were surrounded by most beautifull scenery, and yet could not see it. Towards evening we passed a few pecular shaped lighthouses, and I suppose these put the pilot on the right course, for we instantly went full speed ahead again; and by six O'clock had again anchored. All hands were put over the side to clean

ship, but it came (LIGHTHOUSES IN THE ST. LAWRENCE RIVER)

on to rain, and it had to be put off till next morning The following morn at daybreak; all hands were busily employed clearing the ship side. As soon as this was accomplished, we immediatly got under weigh, and assisted by a strong current made rapid progress up the river, passing the falls of Montmorency on our starboard hand. Just after ten, A.M, we sighted "Quebec," with its magnificent hotels perched upon the heights. By half past ten we were safely moored to a buoy, under the shelter of the Heights of Abraham.

"Quebec."

At Quebec we found the cruisers "Cresent(flag)

"Psyche," "Pallas," "Proserpine," (British) and a French cruiser. When we arrived the heights, were litterally one mass of human beings, and their numbers were swelled a good deal by the time their "Royal Highnesses" left the ship. The weather was fine, but blowing great guns. All the ships were gay with bunting, only one thing

French Cruiser De Estrees.

out of place, admidst these jollyfications; was the half masted "American flag," In memoriam for the late President. Mc Kinley; which was flown by all the warships present. In the afternoon it became overcast, and shortly afterwards the rain fell in sheets, It was nearly as bad as a tropical shower. I expect it was

brought on by the thunder of the saluting
guns; that welcomed the "Duke and Duchess" to
"Canada." But it was a grand sight to see
the quick changes of earth and sky during

this storm, it was like a transformation
scene, hills that were green with verdure
turned black as night, and the dark troubled
waters of the S? Lawrence were turned into
a creamy froth by the force of the gale;
But it passed quickly, and did good after
all, for after it had gone, the wind dropped

which was just what was wanted, as in the
evening, a firework display was to take place
and the fleet to be illuminated. The afforsaid
display was a complete success, one incident
happening, but I dont think anyone was
injured, A Tug boat, that was steaming up
and down the river, discharging fireworks,

PER. MARE   PER TERRAM

ROYAL
MARINE
LIGHT INFANTRY

had a fire break out in
her chart house, owing
I suppose, to the premature
explosion of some of her.
fireworks; she was all
ablaze in an instant, and fireworks flew
about in all directions; to the great danger
of the eye witnesses; Women screamed, and
men lost their heads, & just as it looked as

if a tragedy could not be averted; a couple of
tugs came on the scene and with there steam
hoses, quickly got the fire under control, and
finally put it out altogether. Towards ten o,clock
the sound of singing came from the promenade
up on the heights; it gradually swelled in volume
untill, we, on board the "Ophir," could hear every
word quite, plain they were singing God save the King;
It was good singing, and there must have been
several hundred,s of men and women. taking
part. The following evening, their "Royal
Highnesses and Suite," came on board to
dine, and all the big nobs were invited; we also
had a repetition of the "firework display."
The people here seem to be very fond of
singing, as, about half past nine, a large

pleasure steamer came off to us; and serenaded the "Duke and Duchess" in fine stile, there must have been two or three hundred trained voices present. The next morning Their "Royal Highnesses" again left the ship. and their stay ashore this time would last close on a month; as they had a long journey before them, across the C.P.R. railway I give a program of the places they visited during their journey across "Canada". The next day we took in five hundred tons of coal, and by eight a.m. the next day was under weigh, and escorted by the "Diadem" only, (the "Niobe" remaining behind to coal) were steaming down the river bound for "Halifax"; there to await the return of their "Royal Highnesses".

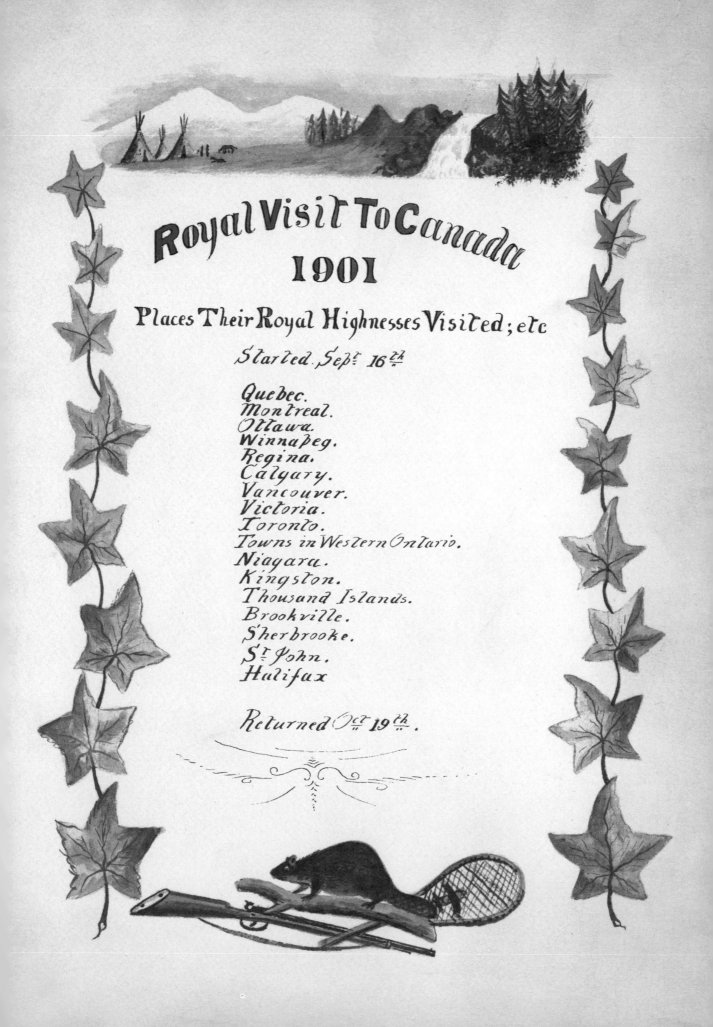

Royal Visit To Canada

1901

Places Their Royal Highnesses Visited; etc

Started, Sept. 16th

Quebec.
Montreal.
Ottawa.
Winnipeg.
Regina.
Calgary.
Vancouver.
Victoria.
Toronto.
Towns in Western Ontario.
Niagara.
Kingston.
Thousand Islands.
Brookville.
Sherbrooke.
St. John.
Halifax

Returned Oct. 19th.

from the western shores of Canada. We made a much better passage down the river than we did coming up, The weather remaining clear and bright, and we were enabled to see some of the beauties of the river. One thing that struck me not only at "Quebec" but all up and down the river, was the amount of churches, the conspictious part of them being their spires, some of them boasting three and one four, there was a grand church; or cathedral, to every few houses, for hundreds of miles on both sides of the river, We passed the island of "Anticosta" sunday morn; and soon after daybreak

on monday morn, we found ourselves in one
of the narrowest and prettiest straits I
had ever passed through; and I was sorry
when we again passed into the open sea.
By seven bells the same afternoon we sighted
the two light houses, that mark the entrance
to the port of "Halifax," An hour afterwards
we were safely moored off a town that,
greatly reminded me of one of our large
midland manufacturing towns; everything
was so black and smoky. The next day a
different kind of routine to what we had
been used to in the "Ophir" commenced. Of
course, as you know we were painted white
and our long sea voyages, had left their

mark, in the shape of rust; streaks and spots putting in an appearance all over the ship; So this morning each man put on his oldest suit, or refitting rig, as it is called; and armed with either a scraper, chipping hammer, or pot of red lead paint and brush, did his best to remove all

the rust, ready for a through painting; which we were going to receive before their "Royal Highnesses" returned to to the ship. In the morning the "Diadem" went up into an inner bay, for torpedo practice, returning to her anchorage by midday. The next day we still continued scraping, painting etc. On the following morning first thing, we slipped from the buoy, and went straight in dock, and as soon as breakfast was over, all hands armed with scrubbers and scrapers, went into the dock, and standing on floating pontoons gave the bottom of the "Ophir" a thorough cleaning, as the water was pumped out; They say that *matelo's are never so happy as when they are up to their knees in water, and they where very happy this day

(*. French slang word for sailor)

and no mistake; cheers, songs, and yells came floating up, from the hundred or more British flat foots, and [*]leathernecks as thir humor guided them. It was a private dock and a large number of civilians gained admittance to have

THE OPHIR IN DOCK AT HALIFAX

a look at the "Ophir," but all their interest

was soon centered on the jovial sailors

under her bottom. After dinner we started

painting her bottom with none fouling

composition; and we only finished by

eight O-clock the same evening. We were

out of dock again by half past six next

morning; and about midday they piped

three days general leave for the starboard

watch, (general leave means everyone except

the very worst of characters can go ashore.)

And I assure you kind reader, it would

not do for any nervous person, to accompany

a party of "British Blues" when on "gem's" ✛

Nothing in the way of sport comes amiss

to them; horse riding, cycling, and driving being the favourites. It would do the people at home good, to see a party of bluejackets on horseback, riding full tear, shouting and yelling like red indians. But I am sorry to say that all their pursuits are not so innocent, as those already mentioned, drunkenness being a very predomenent feature during a general leave; but things are changing for the better, the average man finding he is far better off without the drink. I went on leave saturday night, and came off to the ship again monday morning; and I carried on board very plesant recollections of my short stay on shore. I found it a much better place than it looks. One thing about "Halifax" was they knew how to treat a sailor, when he happened to be partaking of a meal. I say for myself that I never had better meals and the charge was very moderate. Of course being one of the ordinaries. I made tracks for some of the low class drinking dens, and met with an agreeable surprise. The neighbourhood was infested with coloured folks, and judge to my surprise when I found them singing just the same coon songs that were so popular at home, And the same old cake walk was very popular there also. But their singing, and dancing, had a certain pecularity about it, that our professionals in the music halls, could never attain to the life. On the Sunday I with several companions, went a lovely walk through forrest and woodland, and altogether, we all had a very good time off it. We returned to the ship next morning, and the port watch then went on their three days leave. On wednesday the 3rd of Oct— we warped the "Ophir," alongside the coaling jetty; and the next morning, as soon as the watch came back off leave, we started to coal ship, with the help of 60 men from the "Diadem and Niobe." There was a large heap of coal, about a hundred yards from the ship; and it had to be carried inboard in small baskets, holding about half.a.hundred weight; it took us three days to take in eighteen hundred tons; But the men where very cheerfull singing the whole day long; We worked from

six in the morning till nine at night. A continual stream of men entered the ship at one gangway and left by another, some carrying their baskets on their heads, some their backs, whilst some carried them under their arms. Now and then the crowd emerging with empty baskets, would form into a body; and then come come charging, and leaping, and yelling like a lot of savages, on to the coal heap, with sticks for spears, and baskets for shields; We finished late saturday night, and cleaned ship sunday morning. On monday we once more moored up to the buoy in the center of the harbour, and commenced painting and scraping as before detailed. Of course everyone that reads, knows all about their "Royal Highnesses" enthusiastic receptions at all the places they visited, and not a small chapter of adventures fell to their lot. We on board the "Ophir," knew no more about these things than the general public

for our knoledge was gleaned in the same manner
from the Papers

A few objects fast dissapearing from N America

From time to time we were kept in toutch

with "Their Royal Highnesses", by all sorts of

things. arriving; a "Moose's head" came the

other day; said to have been shot by the

"Duke" in the "North West," A tribe of indians have pitched their camp on the shore opposite the ship, and most of them are in full savage dress, it is a most unusual thing to see them thus, they have come to see the "Duke" and must have traveled many hundreds of miles The "Ophir" now looked a picture indeed, not a blemish on her snow white, side whilst her masts and funnels shone like gold in their coating of buff enamel paint. She looked every inch a yacht. a credit to the "Nation" to which she belonged. The "Indefatigable" arrived today She had just come from Quebec, having been tempory repared, after having run aground, up the "St Lawrence;" close to

"Montreal". Two more ships arrived two days after, the "Columbine" and "Alert", these ships had come from the "Newfoundland" fisheries; Two small seccond class torpedo boats were also launched from the slips, these boats were to be used for patroll purposes. when their "Royal Highnesses" arrived

on board. On the 18th of Oct, we left the buoy, and made fast to the coaling

THE CHILDREN'S WELCOME

Sung by the children in welcoming their Royal Highnesses The
Duke and Duchess of Cornwall and York on the Commons. Halifax N.S.

Wolfe the dauntless hero came
And planted firm Britannia's flag
On Canada's fair domain
Here may it wave our boast and pride
And joined in love together
The Thistle, Shamrock, Rose entwine
The Maple Leaf forever

Chorus
The Maple Leaf our emblem dear.
The Maple Leaf forever.
God save our King and Heaven Bless.
The Maple Leaf forever.

On merry England's far famed land
May kind Heaven sweetly smile
God bless old Scotland evermore
And Irelands emerald isle
Then swell the song both loud and long
Till rock and forrest quiver
God save our King and Heaven Bless
The Maple Leaf forever

From every heart a welcome springs
Hearts to home and Britain true
Decendants fair of Stately Kings
We pledge our faith to you
God speed you home with breezes kind
His blessing fail you never
God send ye fadeless keep in mind
The Maple Leaf forever

Chorus
The Maple leaf our emblem dear
The Maple leaf for ever
God send ye fadeless keep in mind
The Maple Leaf for ever

Jetty; Here a great transformation had
taken place, not a sign of coal, or coal dust

H_M_S. CRESENT

being visable anywhere, new boarding was
nailed on the old jetty, and covered with
white sand, and all the sheds were painted
afresh. The town of "Halifax," was also
undergoing a great change, the streets were
ablaze with many coloured flags, and

bunting. There was no need to erect
venetian masts here, as the streets
were lined with
telegraph poles:
that answered
the purpose
admirably.
All the seamen and marines from the
fleet, had been ashore twice, to practice
for the coming review.
An exciting boat
race took place
to day, between the
stokers whalers racing crew of the
Cresent, and a like crew from one of
our escort the Diadem. The Diadem was

the challenger, and after a most exciting race of three miles; in which neither boat seemed to gain; the Diadem's won by an extra spurt, when close on the finishing point; by a length and a half. By all accounts; the betting was heavy on both sides, over two hundred dollars being laid down, so our escort would have a nice bit of money to throw away when we arrived in "Merry England." To morrow was the day for the return of "Their Royal Highnesses"

MAKING A PERIQUE OR PLUG OF NAVY TOBACCO

Loyalty of Red Men

Historic gathering of Alberta indians in war paint and feathers to welcome the Duke & Duchess.

WAR CLOUD
HEAD CHIEFTAIN.

One of the incidents worth mentioning during their "Royal Highnesses" trip across "Canada" was the welcome given by the vast tribes of "Alberta Indians". The scene was a most remarkable one. The Indians were attired in all the panoply of war paint and feathers. Some of them were almost entirely naked, and had their bodies painted in a most remarkable fashion. One Indian mounted upon a fine horse attracted particular attention. He was painted yellow all over, and his cheeks were daubed with vermilion. His horse was

FALLING. STAR.

streaked with yellow ochre, and decorated in a most striking manner with feathers. Some of the Indians were magnificently attired in furs, plumes, and war feathers, and all were painted in a most fantastic manner. The mounted warriors of the various tribes all armed, formed a semi-gordon in front of The "Royal

Party", and inside it the squaws and papooses occupied a position of advantage. The principal chiefs who presented addresses to his Royal Highness, were signed by "White Pup." "Running Rabbit" and "Iron Shield," head chiefs of the "Blackfeet" "Crop ear Wolf" and "Day Wolf" head chiefs of the "Bloods, Running Wolf," chief of the "Piegans, Bulls Head." head chief of the "Sarcees." "Jacob Bears Paw." "John Cheneka," "Jonas Big Stoney" head chiefs of the "Stonies." "Joseph Samson," "Mister Kim." head chiefs of the "Crees." May it please your Royal Highness We, the "Blackfoot, Blood, Piegan, Sarcee, Stony, and Cree Indians" of "Southern Alberta," heartilly welcome your "Royal Highness" to the land of our forefathers. For untold generations our tribes hunted the "Bison" on these plains, as a means of subsistence. But the white man came and desired to settle on our hunting grounds, which were already becoming depleted of their large game; principly by the reckless slaughter of the animals south of the boundry line. Consequently about about aquarter of acentury ago, we accepted the white mans terms, and surrended our lands by treaty to Her late "Majesty "Queen Victoria," whose death we most deeply lament, and of whom you are the illustrious grand-son. On the occasion of this visit, we beg you to convey to your highly-exalted father "King Edward VII." the same expression of devotion to his person, and loyalty to his government, which we promised to his "Royal Mother." The head chiefs of the Indians made the following speeches. "White Pup," head chief of the "Black-feet" told their "Royal Highnesses," that he hoped they would live long on this earth, and said this was the first time he had had the priviledge to meet the Queens grandson. "Crop Ear Wolf," head chief of the "Bloods," presented the treaty made 27 years ago, and he said it was first given to "Red Crow," but after three years it was given to him. For 27 years nothing went wrong with them, when "Queen Victoria" was over them. He never calculated on having the ground he was living on made smaller to him. He said that

"Red crow" told him that when the rivers run dry; that is the time they would get nothing more to eat. He trusted their "Royal Highnesses" would take pity on them. The Queen had

WHITE WOLF
INDIAN BRAVE IN WAR PAINT

never had any wrong words with them. "Jonas Big Stoney" one of the head chiefs of the "Stonies" said though art the great son of a great King and that he was great full to the "Great Spirit" for this occasion, and for giving us this brightening day, and all that is peacefull and Blessed. The sun now above is breaking through the clouds and gladdening us with its presence. This is the first time I have beheld such a gathering of people mingled together in peace and I am thankfull. "Bull Head" said that all the people round want plenty of grub to make them feel happy when they started for home. He said that was the only thing that kept them alive having plenty to eat

The speeches of the Indians, were delivered in a sort of paraphrased singsong; at the very pitch of the voices of the speakers

The Dukes reply

His Royal Highness replied to the Indians in the following Chiefs and men of of the great "Blackfeet" confederation, "Sarcees" and "Stonies" and "Crees". I have listened with much pleasure and satisfaction to your loyal words of greeting. And I shall hasten to convey to my dear father the great "King" your assurances of loyalty and unswerving devotion to him and his government. I thank you very much for the welcome you have given me and the "Duchess" in words that come warm from your hearts. We know of your affection for the beloved "Queen" who is no more. The great mother who loved you so much, and whose loss makes your heart bleed, and the tears to fill your eyes We know this not only from your words, but from the steadfast manner and loyalty you displayed at the time there was trouble in the land; and when ill-advised persons saught to sow disaffection amongst you

They failed to do so. The great King my father still cherishes the remembrance of your fidelity in those days I am glad to learn of the prosperity that now surrounds the Indian teepee, and the beautifull and abundant crops, the heards of cattle, and droves of horses. Those of you who remember the day the "Government of the Great Mother," first came to you, or have heard, or have heard with your ears what your fathers have said, will recollect that your people were often hungry and

wretched, your pipes cold, and your wigwams empty or melancholy. You know that they did not cry to deaf ears The "Great Mother" stretched forth her hands to help you and now those days have passed away, never to return. You may have wants, such is the lot of everyone on this Earth.

But your requests will allways be patiently listened to by those who have been set by the King amongst you. The Indian is a true man his words are true words, and he never breaks faith And he knows that it is the same with the "Great King". His promises last as long as the sun shall shine and the waters flow. And care will ever be taken over you. I have spoken to you as children of our great "Empire". I know that its flag floats or your tents, and that you wear the Kings colors. I feel that your generous hearts have allready told you, that it no mean thing to belong to such an "Empire" and to share in its glories. As you know it is an "Empire" on which the sun never sets. And I wish to assure you that "His Majesty" your great father, has as much love for you of the setting sun, as of his children of the rising sun. We are glad to have seen you We have come a long way, many thousands of miles across the deep waters and vast prairies to see you We will allways remember this day with pleasure, and I will only add a prayer, and that prayer, and that prayer is this. With the help of the "Great Spirit". peace, prosperity, contentment and happiness, may be your lot and rest among you allways. "The King" has ordered a silver medal to be struck, to commemorate the day

And one will be presented to each of the "Head Chiefs" which
shall allways be kept by him as long as he remains in office
and afterwards by his successors. I wish you good bye and hope
you will all return in safety to your homes. After the conclusion
of the address by his "Royal Highness," which was interpreted
to the Indians, The mounted Indians performed a series of
evolutions on horseback which were skilfully executed and
picturesque in effect. Then the Indian children sang "God save
The King" and the "Royal Party" departed for the train.

～～～～ ☀ ～～～～

Their "Royal Highnesses" return to the "Ophir"

It was typical Nova Scotia weather, that their
Royal Highnesses experienced on their
arrival in this Province. As the hour of
arrival grew nearer the crowds outside
the railway depot grew to an enormous

proportion. Shortly before 9.15. a.m. the Viceregal train was reported approaching, and before the scheduled time the train pulled up at the platform. The approach of the "Royal Train" caused a buzz of excitement, as it became known, ending in cheering from the immence concourse, as the rumble of wheels was heard outside. As soon as the train came to a standstill members of the "Royal Party" began to alight, and were welcomed by the "Leiutenant-Governor" and others awaiting their arrival. From the landing platform the "Royal party" proceeded to the platform prepared for the presentation of addresses; being received with prolonged cheering by the immence crowd. At the conclusion of the ceremony Their "Royal Highnesses" decended from the platform and entered their carriage, and the "Royal proccession moved

forward. deffening cheers coming from every
quarter, all along the route, untill they
entered "H. M. Dockyard," right along the
roadway from the dockyard to the "Ophir"
was two lines of Bluejackets one on either
side with drawn cutlass. It was a quiet affair
coming on board; a naval guard of honour was
drawn upon the jetty, but the multitudes
saw nothing of the embarkation, In the afternoon
the "Royal party" again left the ship. The
"Duke" on horseback in the uniform of the
"7th Fusiliers" and the "Duchess" in her carriage
they went to attend a review in which
over "5.000 Bluejacket Marines and Soldiers"
were present. The next day sunday just
after church the whole of the crew went

out on the jetty and had their photo's taken with their "Royal Highnesses" and suite in the foreground

In the afternoon a state luncheon was held on board

The following day was bleak, cold, and dull, the 21st of Oct and the day of our departure from Canada, It was about 9-30 am when we let go our hawsers and the fleet began to slew, bows down the harbour. There were not many people, but they were very enthusiastic and our band played the "Maple Leaf" and several

Just as we commenced to move, the air was filled with falling snow, and it continued, untill we were well out to sea, The fleet now saluted. Turned round and went back with the exception of the "Niobe, Diaden, Cresent, & Proserpine"

LEAVING HALIFAX N.S.

These ships then took up their positions; the "Cresent" a good distance ahead of us, the "Niobe and Diadem," on either side, and the "Proserpine" well astern. The reason of this was, icebergs, dense fogs, etc were common in these latitudes, and being surrounded thus by ships, it was impossible to meet any danger, without timely warning. The weather now was very cold, and snow kept falling from time, to time. At daybreak on the morning of the 23rd Oct we were in sight of "Newfoundland"

St. Johns.
Newfoundland

We entered St. Johns, about 7 a.m. passing in between two high rocky headlands. It was an extremely narrow entrance, and very skillfull navigation was required. On our right as we passed in, these words, high upon the face of the cliff, in large white letters, were very conspicious ("Welcome to Terra Nova"). Inside we found "St Johns" to be a large and flourishing town with several fine buildings, Here we met with "H.M.S. Charybdis", and what we thought

to be more men-of-war, turned out to be steam trawlers, with checkered sides and yellow funnels There was also many hundreds of fishing boats, whalers sealers and cod boats. "Their Royal

"High nesses" did not go ashore till the next day, the 24th. The decorations etc were extremely good, taking into consideration the elements, which were cold wet and windy; there were several fine arches and the poorest houses had their show of decoration.

A PRESENT FROM NEWFOUNDLAND TO THE YOUNG PRINCE EDWARD

"The Royal Party" was very well received on landing, the people cheering themselves hoarse. Amongst the presents received by their "Royal Highnesses, was a "Newfoundland" dog harnessed to a small mailcart. The dog was a beauty, and although only nine months old, was nearly as strong as a man. This present was for young "Prince Edward" "Their Royal Highnesses" eldest son. Both nights during our stay here, the town and fleet illuminated, there was also fire work displays, whilst high upon the rocky mounts, burnt huge bonfires. "The Royal Party" did not stay ashore very long, as the weather was wretched. The next morning about 6 O-clock the "Cresent. Niobe and Diadem" weighed anchor and one by one, proceeded out to sea. Below I give some

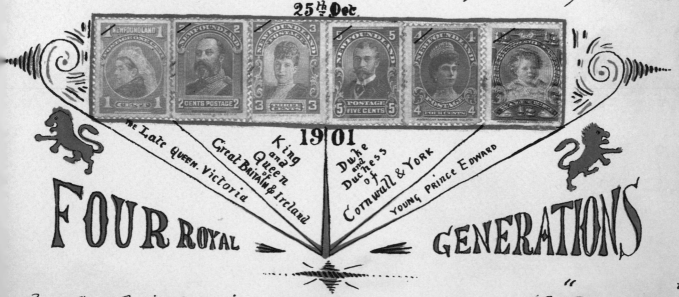

25th Oct

1901

The Late Queen. Victoria — King and Queen of Great Britain & Ireland — Duke and Duchess of Cornwall & York — Young Prince Edward

FOUR ROYAL GENERATIONS

stamps, printed in commemoration of "The Royal Visit"

Homeward Bound.

The Cresent bidding us farewell with her 6ᵗʰ Guns

It was about 7. a.m, by the time we cast off from the jetty, and we immediatly steamed out to sea, and picked up with our escort, "The Cresent" steaming ahead of us. About 9. a.m she steamed round in a circle, and came close up along side of us, her crew manned ship and afterwards manned the rigging. Her band then played the "King," and then "Home sweet home", "Auld lang syne", and "Rolling Home to merry England". Her crew mean while giving

us three hearty cheers which we returned. She then
began to shear off, and drop astern; saluting at the
same time with her 6" quick firing guns. We at once
went full speed ahead and soon the "Cresent" was a
speck on the horizon. The "Diadem" was ordered to
go on ahead, and report any ships etc. A cold wet wind
was blowing from the N.E., and about midnight

she reported an iceberge off our port bow, and
soon afterwards played her search light full upon
it. We passed it quite close, by its appearance it
looked as if it had been floating about some time
the sides of it being quite smooth. It was a beautifull

sight but a terrible danger to shipping, especially in misty or foggy weather, but it took but a short time to dissappear from view at the rate we were traveling. All the men were in great glee at the prospect of soon being in "Old England" once more. "Portsmouth" was looked forward to with more interest than any place we had been to yet; and sea songs, mostly about going home, were the order of the day, and night. "Rolling Home to Merry England," being the favourite. And without a doubt we were "rolling home, for with an heavy sea on our beam, we were rolling to a considerable extent, and continued to do so, for four or five days, untill we arrived off the coast of "Ireland" when the sea subsided a good deal On the morning of the 30ᵗʰ at daybreak we sighted a lot of ships right ahead; which turned out to be the "Channel Squadron", comprising six battle ships, the "Magnificent,"(flag) "Majestic," (flag) "Jupiter," "Mars," "Hannibal," and "Prince George," and six cruisers. the "Arrogant," "Furious,"

SIGHTING THE CHANNEL FLEET.

"Hyacinth," "Minerva," and our old escort the "St George and Juno." The battleships being on the right, the cruisers to the left, But they soon formed up and began to steam slowly in the same direction as us; being, some six miles ahead of us. About eight. p.m, they turned about and

H.M.S. "MAGNIFICENT" IN WAR PAINT

came bearing down on us full speed, in two lines, or subdivisions line ahead. When they got quite close, one line swung round to starboard and one to port of us; and then forming up into two long lines; one each side flagships leading. Whilst this evolution was being carried out the whole fleet saluted. It was a grand spectacle, and no mistake about it, to see these 15.000 ton fighting machines at play. It does not do to ponder, and think what the scene would look like if these monsters of the deep, was to meet in deadly combat. One thing surprised us all; That was finding the "Magnificent" in full war paint black and grey, and she looked much more formidable than if she was painted in

the ordinary Naval colours of black, white,
yellow, and red. By eleven, p.m. we were
off "Lands End." In the middle watch a
stiff head wind sprang up, and soon afterwards
it was blowing half a gale. Daylight next
morning opened up a splendid scene to view.
We were just off "Plymouth." the sea a mass
of foam with the force of the wind, and
the long line of battleships and cruisers on
either side of us, were throwing up sheets
of spray right over their funnels. I could
make out most of the places, "Salcombe,"
"Dartmouth," "Torquay," etc, as we made our
way up channel, then we lost sight of the

THE OPHIR LEADING THE CHANNEL FLEET.

land again. About 11. a.m. we sight "Portland Pill," our arrangements were to anchor here till the next day, but the weather was so unfavourable that we continued on our way, being joyned by the "Pactolus" second class cruiser with mails About half past 2 in the afternoon we passed the "Needles" "Isle of Wight" and soon afterwards

THE NEEDLES ISLE OF WIGHT.

dropped anchor in comparativly smooth water. In the afternoon about half past four, their "Royal Highnesses" presented the officers and crew with a small medallion as a souvenir of the cruise, the officers being

of gold and the mens silver In the evening

SHOWING BOTH SIDES OF THE MEDAL
PRESENTED TO THE OFFICERS & MEN.
OF
H. M. S. "OPHIR"
BY T. R. H.
DUKE & DUCHESS OF CORNWALL & YORK

a dinner party was held on board, Honouring

the officers of the "Channel Fleet." The next

morning about six the whole of the fleet except

the "St George, & Juno", got under weigh, and proceeded

to "Spithead." About 10·30. a.m. the "New Royal

Yacht" accompanied by the "Trinity Yacht Irene"

was seen approaching; the "Royal Yacht" had

the standard flying, showing that their Majesty's

were on board. As they drew closer we manned

ship, and the "St George and Juno" saluted with

their six inch guns. The "Royal Yacht Victoria"

and Albert came up right abrest of us

and let go her anchor

Home Sweet Home.
the
King and Queen

and the People's welcome home.

THE ROYAL YACHT "VICTORIA & ALBERT"

As soon as possible a steam boat was

lowered from the "Royal Yacht," and was

soon on its way to the "Ophir" with their

"Majesty's" on board. They came up alongside the starboard gangway but the water was so choppy that they could not get aboard; so the "Duke and Duchess", and suite, went down the ladder as far as possible. The King looked very

MAST HEAD FLAGS OF THE "OPHIR"

"PRINCE OF WALES" STANDARD   "TRINITY HOUSE FLAG"

happy indeed, The "Queen" was in the cabin, but he caught her by the arm, and said come out and let them have a look at you. "The Duke's children" were in the boat too, and were eager to catch a glimse of their "Royal Parents", "Young Prince Edward" came scrambling between the King's legs to have first look. They did not remain alongside long, but waved adieu for the time, and went alongside the "Victoria and Albert," were they had a specially fitted gangway in case of a rough sea. "Commodore Lambton of Ladysmith" fame was in charge of the boat. About two o-clock in the afternoon, we all weighed anchor and with the "Irene" leading and the "St George and Juno" bring up the rear we steamed slowly up the "Solent," before long we were surrounded by pleasure boats, steamers, crowded with enthusiastic people, who cheered themselves hoarse, After passing Cowes on the right we came to the fleet anchored in two lines

They saluted us, just before we reached them and each ships company gave us three cheers as we passed them. After passing through the lines, we were hove to for a few minutes to allow the "Royal Yachts" to enter and get berthed first. But we soon went ahead again, the shores on

THE SEARCHLIGHTS OF THE FLEET

both sides of the harbour, were black with people, and despite the strong breeze blowing their cheers could be plainly heard. As we got closer in, the cheering was simply deffening and what with the bands ashore, and our band playing "Home sweet Home," it made a home coming never to be forgotten. As we passed in between the narrow entrance to the harbour, with the forts, and houses etc, clothed with people, the fleet saluted; included the old "Victory," and the scores of steam pleasure boats, kept up a continual din with their hooters. We soon drew up to the same old jetty we left several months back. Here a naval

H.M.S. "VICTORY".

guard was drawn up, and they gave us

three rousing cheers waving their staw hats

mean while—. We were soon made fast and

the gangway got out, and then as soon as

possible the "Dukes" suite ran ashore, and

there was much exciting talk and handshakings

"Their Royal Highnesses" left the ship soon

after wards, and went aboard the "Victoria

and Albert," we did not witness the meeting

with the "King, Queen, and children". In the

evening a grand dinner was held on board

the Kings yacht, the "Ophir's" band attending

During the speeches made at dinner the

King said this was the happiest day he

had spent this year. Right through the

evening up till midnight all men of war
illuminated; the "Victory" made a unique
spectacle for between her for and main
mast triced high up, like a sky sign, was
the words (Welcome home) in golden electric
lights; a torpedo boat destroyer, berthed

THE "VICTORY"   ILLUMINATED

along side of her, supplied the motor
power. Out at "Spithead" the Channel
Fleet looked grand, clothed with electricity,

Welcome. Home.

Welcome and hail! In the moment of meeting,
First on the shore, by the edge of the foam.
Surely the people may offer the greeting,
Welcoming Prince and Princess to their home.

Long was the journey, the whole earth embracing,
Passing through every climate and zone,
Yet it was merely the boundaries tracing,
Marking the Empire that travels alone.

What says the proverb, of him who shall travel? —
He who goes lonely shall travel afar.
Britain perchance may the problem unravel,
Lonely she rides in her conquering car

Allies we need not, and foemen we need not,
Everywhere flutters the flag of our birth
Nations are blind, if the riddle they read not
Britain rides lonely, the Queen of the Earth

Hush for a moment, a father and mother,
Claim the first greeting of daughter and son.
Then the whole Nation shall offer another,
Joyful to know, that the journey is done

Yet it was only the lord of the manor,
Sending his heir, to look round the estate.
Starting from home with the family banner,
Welcomed to day once again at the gate.
———— '' ————

Only his land is an Empire extending,
Over the world, and maintaining her sway
Eastward and westward in glory unending,
Sunlit through every hour of the day
———— '' ————

Home from the tropical haunts of the tiger,
Home from the regions of iceberg and snow.
Home from the lands, where the Nile and the Niger,
Form but new paths, where our sailors must go.
———— '' ————

Home from the Commonwealth proud of her glory,
Land of the duckbill, dingo, kangaroo.
Latest to add, to the Empires great story
One more new chapter, as strange as its true
———— '' ————

Home then at last! Now the journey is ended
Gladly we welcome you back to the shore
After a run through an empire so splendid
All that we ask is to leave us no more
———— '' ————

Hopeful we greet you our prayers addressing,
To him who rules over all things above.
May he upon you, pour every Blessing,
Guiding you ever in wisdom and love.

————·······——((<⇔>))——·······————

After their return the "Duke & Duchess."
received the titles of "Prince & Princess of Wales"
and they were entertained by the "Lord Mayor
of London", at a banquet in the "Guildhall
on the "5th December 1901."
The following is taken from a speech made
by his "Royal Highness". It may interest
you to know that although we travelled over
forty five thousand miles; (With the exception of
Port Said) we never set foot on any land where
the "Union Jack" did not wave. (Loud & prolonged applause
If I were asked to specify any particular

impression derived from our journey. I should
at once place before all others that of loyalty
to the "Crown", and attachment to the old
country, by our "Colonists". It was indeed touching
to hear the invariable references to "Home"
Even from the lips of those who never had been,
nor were ever likely to be in these islands.
In this loyalty, lies the strength of a true
and living membership, in the great & glorious
                    "British Empire"

THE ROYAL TOUR
1901

GIBRALTAR
MALTA
ADEN
EGYPT
INDIA
CEYLON
SINGAPORE
AUSTRALIA
NEW
ZEALAND
TASMANIA
MAURITIUS

SOUTH
AFRICA
ST.HELENA
ASCENCION
QUEBEC
ACROSS
CANADA
VANCOUVER
NIAGARA
FALLS
NEW
FOUNDLAND

'H.M.R.Y. OPHIR.'
WITH ESCORT NIOBE & DIADEM
DISTANCE COVERED OVER 50 THOUSAND MILES

13 The Impact of Europe

Sequestered in the Forbidden City, China's rulers rarely received foreigners. The audience that Emperor T'ung Chih granted to foreign envoys in 1873 (above) was the last imperial reception until 1889.

In 1514 an Italian navigator in the service of Portugal, Rafael Perestrello, landed at Canton, having traveled to that harbor from the Portuguese base at Malacca on the Malay Peninsula. The Ming dynasty had been on the throne for one hundred forty-six years, and about eighty years had passed since the great Ming maritime expeditions had explored the Indian Ocean. Perestrello, who had arrived aboard a Chinese ship, acted circumspectly; his successors came in Portuguese vessels, and most of them were less cautious. They behaved with arrogance and violence, and were driven away by local authorities, who thought of them as pirates. Nonetheless, these uncouth mariners were the harbingers of the greatest transformation that the Chinese civilization was to experience in the three thousand years of its history—a transformation that has achieved its complete development only in our own time, more than four hundred years after Perestrello reached Canton.

For nearly a century the only contact between Europe and China was through Portuguese traders. Toward the end of the sixteenth century, Roman Catholic missionaries came out to China with the merchant adventurers. Matteo Ricci, the first successful missionary, landed in 1582, and nineteen years later was permitted to establish himself in Peking. He brought to China the scholarship as well as the piety and devotion of Christian Europe. He was well received by the Chinese, whose language he learned and whose conventions he respected. One scholar-official, observing the similarity of his activities to those of the Buddhist monks who came to China from India in the T'ang period, recommended that Ricci be given the same treatment: the court should not grant exceptional favors to the foreign priest, but should tolerate him so long as he behaved with prudence and moderation. When it was found that Ricci and his successors understood more mathematics than Chinese astronomers did, and that they were able to predict eclipses and other such phenomena more accurately than the Chinese, they were regarded even more favorably, and their scientific talents were employed. It was Western science, not Western religion, that opened the door to cultural contact.

Unlike the Jesuits, the traders and navigators were treated with deep suspicion and hedged with many restrictions, which often were imposed upon them in reaction to their unruly and violent conduct. The Portuguese had come from strongholds that they had already established in India. They had won these strongholds by force, and they expected to do the same in China. They took no account of the fact that whereas India was politically fragmented, imperial China was strongly unified. The Portuguese were repulsed, and when they were allowed back to trade, they were confined to the isolated anchorages of Macao and Amoy. The disrepute they had acquired was shared by the Dutch and later by the English, and to some degree by European voyagers from every nation. Europeans were known as the *Yang Kuei-tzŭ*, or "Ocean Devils"; the term remained in widespread use until modern times. The fact that the demons of the Buddhist hell were often depicted with red hair and green or blue eyes helped to confirm this satanic view of the Western visitors, many of whom had fair hair and light eyes.

Still, trade was profitable. The foreigners bought tea, silk, and porcelain, and generally paid for them with silver, since their own wares were little valued in China. In the early period of contact with the West, the balance of trade was wholly in China's favor, and so was the balance of influence brought about by trade. The Europeans drank tea and prized Chinese porcelain; silk was all the fashion. They also found that rhubarb, a Chinese medicinal herb, was very good for the digestion. (Later a chauvinistic Chinese official was to suggest to his emperor that one way to deal with the troublesome English would be to forbid the export of rhubarb; the foreigners would then be incapacitated by the costive effects of their heavy diet.) The word that is used all over the world for tea, and the words for silk in every European language, are of Chinese origin. "China" or "chinaware" are the common terms for porcelain.

While the seafaring nations of western Europe were establishing trading relations along the southern coast of China, other Westerners—the Russians—were rapidly approaching China's northern frontier. In the sixteenth century the Russian empire expanded east of the Urals. By 1644 the Russians had established the long route across Siberia and encamped on the Amur River, which now forms part of the frontier between the Soviet Union and China. Although the Russians apparently did not know it, the newly established Manchu dynasty, which had come to power that very same year, asserted a claim to the left bank of the Amur up to the Stanovoi mountain chain. The land was wild and hardly inhabited, but such tribes as roamed it acknowledged the Manchu monarch as their sovereign. A frontier clash in 1652, which was won by the Russians, was followed by strong Manchu reprisals; but eventually the Russians and Chinese decided that peace between them could be honorably agreed upon. In 1689 a treaty was signed at the Russian settlement of Nerchinsk; in 1727 this treaty was amplified by another agreement signed at Kyakhta on the Mongolian border.

One of the consequences of the Treaty of Nerchinsk was that the Russians were allowed to set up an Eastern Orthodox mission in Peking to look after the spiritual needs of a group of Cossacks who had been captured

during the border war. These men and their dependents had been moved to Peking and were not allowed to return to Russian territory after the signing of peace. The community has survived until modern times, but is now almost entirely Chinese in race. The religious mission that was set up provided the czars with a useful semiofficial link with the Chinese government, for in imperial Russia the Church was very dependent on the State. Priests sent to Peking could make contact with high Manchu officials; they provided the Russian imperial government with an inconspicuous representative in Peking many years before western European nations even attempted to establish a resident minister there.

The difference in treatment accorded to China's great land neighbor and that meted out to the seafaring nations merits consideration. Siberia, although contiguous with territories of the Manchu empire, was far from Peking and very remote from St. Petersburg—at least before the trans-Siberian railway was built. Russian outposts on the almost-uninhabited borderland did not appear to pose a threat. Furthermore, Russian trade with China, which in the early period consisted almost ex-

clusively of the exchange of Siberian furs for Chinese tea, was a trade that involved the interests and comforts of the ruling class. Therefore the traders were treated with more consideration than western European traders were. Another factor in the favorable treatment of the Russians was that the Manchu emperors were familiar with them. K'ang Hsi, Yung Chêng, and Ch'ien Lung, whose reigns covered the first one hundred fifty years of the dynasty, had all campaigned in the far north. No emperor had even so much as visited China's southern provinces or embarked on the ocean, even for a pleasure cruise.

While the Russians and Chinese were establishing congenial relations, western European merchants were chafing under Chinese restrictions on trade. They had been confined to the single port of Canton during the Ming dynasty and remained so confined throughout the rest of the seventeenth century and all of the eighteenth. The Opium War of 1840 changed this situation. In the eighteenth century the British, who were in control of India, discovered that opium, which could be grown in their vast colony, was being used in China for medicinal purposes. The East India Com-

IDES, *Three Years Travel from Moscow Overland to China*, LONDON, 1706

pany, which monopolized British trade with China, began exporting opium and in 1750 sold 400 chests, each of which weighed roughly 133 pounds. The opium habit spread rapidly, soon tilting the balance of trade against China. At last the Europeans had found something the Chinese would buy. The rise of the opium trade is eloquently recorded: in 1821, 5,000 chests were imported; by 1839, on the eve of the Opium War, this figure had risen to 30,000 chests. By that time the outflow of Chinese silver to pay for the drug amounted to one hundred million ounces.

Alarmed by the loss of revenue and by the evil consequences of the opium habit, the Manchu government forbade the drug's importation as early as 1800. The East India Company complied with this law, but winked at the trade that was still carried on by so-called country ships—British ships registered in India—claiming that these ships did not come under the control of the East India Company. The opium was stored in hulks moored offshore in the estuary of the Pearl River below Canton. Chinese importers agreed on terms with the British merchants in Canton, and then took delivery straight from the hulks.

No duty was paid, for opium was now an illegal import. This was open smuggling, but since the local officials received a large share of the profits for averting their eyes, the trade continued, "unseen" and unchecked.

The evils flowing from the trade had become obvious. Apart from the damage done to the health of those who overindulged (probably a small minority), the economy suffered from the outflow of silver. Taxes had to be paid in silver; but most people earned their wages in humble copper currency, and the rate of exchange between copper and silver was not fixed. As silver grew scarcer, the value of copper fell, and more copper cash was needed to buy an ounce of silver. Tax revenues fell, prices rose, and the burden on the poor increased heavily.

The Emperor Tao Kuang was a man of some goodwill and considerable parsimony. He decided to put an end to the illegal trade because the state was losing too much money and opium was harming the health of the people. The task was entrusted to an honest and upright official, Lin Tsê-hsü, whom the modern Chinese see as something of a hero—although in their eyes he still suffers from the

One provision of the Treaty of Nerchinsk, signed by Russia and China in 1689, was that a Russian trading caravan would be permitted to cross Chinese territory and enter Peking every three years—a privilege that was denied the other European trading nations. This eighteenth-century British view pictures the first Russian delegation, led by Peter the Great's unofficial ambassador to China, nearing a gate in the Great Wall in 1692.

Before 1840 all foreign trade with China was conducted through the lone Treaty Port of Canton, where government-franchised trading monopolies—known as hongs—*bargained with representatives of the equally monopolistic British East India Company. The flags of several foreign trading nations fly over the waterfront warehouses of the* hong *merchants in this nineteenth-century British painting.*

limitation of being a "bourgeois official." Lin confiscated huge stocks of opium that were stored ready for sale and had them publicly destroyed. The British could not complain directly about the destruction of illegal goods, but they did demand compensation for their loss. Lin refused. Such were the origins of the Opium War of 1840. Ill-prepared for the war, especially at sea, China was defeated and forced to sign the Treaty of Nanking in 1842, the first of the so-called Unequal Treaties. Its signing ended the beginning phase of contact with the West. The era of the Treaty Ports began, to endure for almost exactly a century.

The first phase of contact with the West—the period from the sixteenth century to the Opium War—had been a time of varying fortune for the Christian missions in China. Early in the eighteenth century the conduct of the Jesuit missionaries, until then the only Catholic missionaries in China, was criticized by newly arrived Dominicans, who claimed that the tolerant Jesuits permitted converts to vener-

ate ancestral tablets and set off fire crackers during solemn ceremonies, such as Mass, thus continuing practices that were really pagan. The Jesuits countered that these were merely local customs, without true religious content, and therefore were permissible. The Rites Controversy dragged on for many years, with appeals and counterappeals made to successive popes. The Manchu Emperor K'ang Hsi, offended that any "barbarian chief"—as he termed the pope—would dare to interfere in the affairs of China, prohibited all Christian missionaries from teaching, although he utilized the scientific skills of some of the more learned priests. The Rites Controversy greatly damaged the Christian cause in China and inhibited intellectual contact between China and Western civilization. The converts were not all lost; indeed, many remained faithful to Christianity. But the number of learned European priests was greatly reduced, and the priests who remained in the country were no longer allowed easy contact with their Chinese colleagues.

The Christian missionaries, who had been tolerated as the exponents of a harmless foreign fashion, were now suspected of being merely a cover for the designs of alien powers. The history of the nineteenth century was to confirm and deepen this suspicion. Whereas the early Roman Catholic missionaries were concerned solely with the spiritual condition of the Chinese people, many of the nineteenth-century Protestant missionaries tended to be very much interested in the trade their countrymen hoped to do in China. This may have been a by-product of missionary experience in India and Indonesia, where the Moslem and Hindu religions daunted many a missionary. In 1807 Robert Morrison, a Scottish Protestant, reached Canton and started a lone evangel under great difficulties and by clandestine methods. A few years later, under the terms of the Treaty of Nanking, missionaries of all denominations were, in theory, allowed to enter China freely, to purchase property, and to conduct their work unhindered. In

practice, however, they met with great hostility and passive resistance. They did not escape the stigma of having gained a foothold in China through their governments' military power.

At this time almost all Europeans firmly believed that the Chinese or any other Asian people could rise on the scale of material civilization only by adopting Christianity. In the eighteenth century European scholars, such as Voltaire, who had read the learned Jesuits' translations of Chinese classical literature and philosophy, were filled with admiration for the civilization of China, which seemed to them superior in many ways to the system under which they themselves lived. For them China became an idealized land of wise sages and cultivated scholars, where poetry, philosophy, and art were the proper activities of gentlemen, and war was left to rough and rude soldiers of inferior social standing. The Jesuit account of China was based in part on idealistic Chinese traditions and in part on a truthful appreciation of the power and per-

Although trade with the Chinese was highly profitable, it was also highly exasperating. Confined during business hours to the foreign "factories" (above) on a narrow strip of land outside Canton, foreign traders were forced to return to Macao as soon as their business was done. Contact with Chinese officials was prohibited, and members of the merchants' own families were restricted to nearby Macao.

343

A British steamship, appropriately named the Nemesis, *fires on a fleet of junks during the Opium War.*

sonal qualities of emperors such as K'ang Hsi and his grandson Ch'ien Lung. The history of these virtuous rulers, each of whom reigned for many years, also served to reinforce among Europeans the belief in Chinese longevity—a belief that accorded with the Chinese ideal of a long life. The scholars of eighteenth-century Europe, who lived amid the turmoil of a multitude of hostile kingdoms, were impressed too by the huge size and the perfect internal peace that reigned in the great empire during most of this period. After the Opium War, however, these attitudes fell wholly out of fashion. China was considered poor, backward, heathen, ill-governed, obstinately proud, and, above all, militarily weak, a sin that every state must at all costs avoid.

Lord Macartney, who was the first English ambassador to China and who in the year 1793 wrote an account of his embassy, was one of the first to perceive that all was not well in the Manchu empire. Macartney, sent by King George III to the court of the aged Emperor Ch'ien Lung, was impressed by the extent of the imperial control, by the wealth of the court, and by the luxury of the Manchu nobility. But, in the course of his long journey from Canton to Peking and back, he also saw the poverty of the people, the corruption of low-ranking officials, and the ruling class' indifference to and ignorance of any foreign innovation or invention. Macartney had brought some of the latest European scientific instru-

ments as gifts to the court. They were regarded as toys, amusing but without great interest or significance. The court matched its contempt for modernity with political arrogance. The emperor would not consider the idea of equal diplomatic relations with Britain; he refused to ease restrictions on trade and treated the embassy like a tribute-bearing mission from Korea or Nepal—that is, he was very generous with gifts but totally adamant in his rejection of political innovation or trade expansion.

The diplomatic impasse continued well into the nineteenth century. The Manchu emperors based their position on the attitudes and claims of dynasties that had ruled centuries before, when such attitudes were quite justified. Intellectual contact had withered with the Rites Controversy, and trade contact was continually disrupted by disputes and quarrels, which were exacerbated by the extortionate practices of officials at Canton. Diplomatic contact failed to break through the barriers of outmoded customs and attitudes.

As a consequence of the Opium War and the Treaty of Nanking, however, trade was active, despite frequent disruptions. The United States and France concluded their own treaties with China in 1844. They were granted extraterritorial jurisdiction over their own citizens and the privilege of a fixed five per cent tariff on everything they exported to China. French and American missionaries were allowed to preach and travel, to purchase property, and to reside in the interior. France availed itself of the right to establish residential concessions at the Treaty Ports; the United States did not.

It is a curious fact that the rights yielded at Nanking were seen quite differently then than they are now. To the foreigner, security of life and property under his own laws and within his own residential concession was the great gain. The Chinese of the official class, on the other hand, thought these affairs trifling matters of convenience, which they were glad to delegate to foreigners, saving themselves the troubles of direct jurisdiction over fractious aliens. But they were shocked by all efforts to set up legations in Peking, and they strongly resisted these efforts. They disliked the free activity of missionaries, considering them subversive. They were, however, quite content with the limited tariff, for at least the money that was brought in went to the imperial government and not to local officials.

Later Chinese viewed the Unequal Treaties in a way that is exactly contrary. Concessions and extraterritorial jurisdiction are seen as monstrous imperialist invasions of China's sovereignty and dignity; and tariff limitation, an outright exploitation of a weak, "semi-colonial" China. On the other hand, the missionaries, although sometimes tactless, are recognized as having been generally beneficial, since they introduced new techniques and knowledge, particularly in the field of medicine. In any case, their religious activities are seen as largely ineffectual and therefore of secondary importance. The exchange of diplomatic representatives between China and other countries is recognized as a welcome, modern advance, and the court is considered wrong to have opposed it. The indemnity of twenty-one million ounces of silver exacted by the British in the Treaty of Nanking is considered a gross act of plunder that weighed most heavily on the poor, forced up taxes, and led to increasing weakness and internal disorder.

In this last assessment posterity is surely right. In 1850, less than ten years after the Treaty of Nanking, the great T'ai P'ing Rebellion broke out. In many respects it can be considered a direct result of the Opium War. Its leader, Hung Hsiu-ch'üan, was from the Canton region and was a member of an underprivileged local minority, the Hakka. Hung

failed to pass the civil service examination; he became very ill, and during his sickness he had a vision that he later imagined as an interview with God in Heaven. In it God gave him the mission to destroy demons (identified as the Manchu rulers) and to institute the reign of true religion and peace. Hung's chance reading of a Protestant tract, in which he found a partial explanation of the dogmas and teachings of reformed Christianity, seemed to confirm his vision; it led him to believe that Christianity, as he understood it, was divinely revealed religion. Hung became a convert to Christianity. In a brief interview at Canton with an American missionary, Issachar Roberts, he asked to be baptized. Roberts did not believe him yet fit to receive the sacrament; the rejection did not diminish Hung's enthusiasm or shake his conviction. He gathered followers, who became his ardent disciples, and founded the Society of God Worshipers. He also moved to another Hakka settlement in the next province, Kuangsi, probably because his new views were

Pictured above are two of the millions of addicted citizens who smoked opium, or "black gold," on a debilitating and, in most cases, daily basis in China.

not well received in his native district.

In 1851, having clashed with the local officials as a result of their acts of vandalism against Buddhist and Taoist temples, the God Worshipers rose in rebellion. In October of that year, at the small city of Yung-an in Kuangsi, they proclaimed the establishment of the *T'ai P'ing T'ien Kuo*, the "Great Heavenly Peaceful Kingdom," as it is usually translated. (It has been pointed out, however, that *p'ing* means both "level" and "equal" as well as "peace." The "Heavenly Kingdom of Complete Equality" is also a possible translation, and perhaps comes nearer to the meaning.)

In Hung's view all men who worshiped God were equal, even if some were given the duty and right of leadership. The question of how far these ethical and spiritual factors counted in the T'ai P'ing movement is still much disputed. It is certain that to Hung and some of the earlier leaders these beliefs were real; to many of their followers they were cherished sacred dogmas; to great numbers of later recruits to the rebellion they were unintelligible.

Almost from the first the movement gained rapid success, and great numbers of men were enrolled in it. There were reasons for this that had nothing to do with religion. The Opium War and the opening to foreign trade of ports such as Shanghai and Ning-po near the outlet of the Yangtze had resulted in the diversion of the silk, porcelain, and tea trade from Canton. Formerly these export goods had to be carried south by porters, over the mountain ranges that separate Kiangsi province from Kuangtung. Now, however, these goods could be carried to the new Treaty Ports along inland waterways, and huge numbers of porters and other transport workers in the south were thrown out of work and into desperate poverty. Furthermore, the people of south China had always been, at best, lukewarm supporters

of the dynasty. The Manchus remained alien to the south; they spent most of their lives, and the revenues of the empire, in Peking.

The first shock wave of rebellion carried all before it. Advancing north through Hunan (although failing to take its capital, Ch'angsha), the T'ai P'ing rebels sailed down the Yangtze, appearing before Nanking, the southern capital, in March, 1853. They took this city, and there Hung, who styled himself the "Heavenly King," set up the permanent capital of his regime. He would not take the Chinese title of *Huang Ti*, which is translated as "emperor," for he thought it was only appropriate for God. At his court there were no eunuchs; women were given rights unheard of in Chinese society. Footbinding was outlawed. Many other reforms were projected and proclaimed, but the exigencies of war prevented their implementation. Nevertheless, the T'ai P'ing program did represent a significant movement of social reform as well as religious innovation.

Had the T'ai P'ings followed up their victory at Nanking with an immediate advance, in strength, on Peking, the Manchu empire would probably have collapsed. Instead, the rebels made the mistake of sending only a small and weakly supported force; it nonetheless reached a point only eighty miles from the capital before hastily-rallied imperial forces and the approach of the harsh northern winter forced a retreat. Thereafter, the war dragged on in the Yangtze valley for eleven years, with varying degrees of success and failure for the rebels.

A major result of the prolonged struggle was that the Manchus were compelled to rely for defense on new Chinese-manned, Chinese-led armies, raised by loyal officials in the Yangtze provinces. In time these forces wore down the T'ai P'ing resistance, and internal quarrels in 1856 weakened T'ai P'ing morale.

Yet even in the early 1860's under Li Hsiu-Ch'eng, a commander of integrity and ability, the T'ai P'ing rebels were still able to invade the eastern provinces, capture Su-chou and Hang-chou, and threaten Shanghai. The Europeans in Shanghai defended themselves by enlisting an army of adventurers, at first commanded by Frederick Townsend Ward, an American, and after his death by the British General Charles Gordon ("Chinese" Gordon, later of Khartoum fame). Eventually, Chinese armies loyal to the emperor closed in on Nanking, which fell in July, 1864. The "Heavenly King" died of natural causes a few weeks before the end of the rebellion.

In the years after the rebellion, the government inaugurated a cautious policy of reform and modernization, the first undertaken by any Manchu government. The reforms constituted a major step toward a modern society—not that modernization itself was their intention. They hoped to make China strong enough to resist pressure from foreign powers. They did not foresee that in the very process of trying to build up Chinese strength they had to educate a new generation that would radically depart from traditional Chinese ideals.

After a long struggle to end rebellion, China was still confronted with the manifest power and aggressive attitudes of foreign powers, who had profited from the recent turmoils to exact further servitudes and cessions from the harassed empire. In 1856 the Western powers attacked China once more, while the country was still in the throes of the T'ai P'ing Rebellion. The British were dissatisfied with the meager results of the Treaty of Nanking, the continuing hostility of the population, and the obstructions of officials in the Treaty Ports. As a pretext for their assault, Britain and France seized on a trifling incident—the arrest by Chinese police of fourteen Chinese crewmen of the *Arrow*, a small ship of British regis-

try. It was the type of incident that would hardly rate a diplomatic note in later times, but the European response was a blockade of Canton and the bombardment and capture of the city.

The war was then carried north by sea to the mouth of the Pei River, which connects Tientsin, the port of Peking, with the sea. In May, 1858, the allied fleets bombarded and took the forts guarding the river mouth at Taku. In June the Manchu court, harried by the T'ai P'ing war and other rebellions, agreed to a new treaty. Eleven more Treaty Ports were opened to trade, and it was positively stipulated that foreign envoys could reside in Peking. The Yangtze was opened to foreign shipping for hundreds of miles up to Hank'ou. Four million ounces of silver were exacted as an indemnity, although it was not apparent that either Britain or France had suf-

fered any damages from this war.

No one today would deny that the Arrow War was naked aggression. For the Chinese it is the major example of imperialism in action, and they have not forgotten it. The year after the treaty was signed they tried to repudiate it; when the British fleet returned to Taku, the Chinese successfully repulsed a second attempt on the forts. The British and French returned in force in 1860, took Tientsin, and moved on Peking, which they captured in September. Emperor Hsien Fêng fled to Jehol in Inner Mongolia, where before long he died. He left behind his brother, Prince Kung, to negotiate a still more degrading treaty with the victorious invaders.

Not only seafaring nations saw that the time had come for a fresh advance. In the far north the Russians were once again active. In 1854 a new and vigorous Russian governor-

Disputes over territorial rights in Korea, dating from the seventh century A.D., *led to the Sino-Japanese War of* 1894. *Following a series of clashes, one of which is pictured in the Japanese print at left, China signed a humiliating treaty that ensured Korea's "independence." Japan waited only fifteen years before formally annexing the country.*

general, Count Nikolai Muraviëv, sailed down the Amur to its mouth, exploring the area along the banks. The next year he quietly put Russia in control of the whole trans-Amur region, which had been recognized as Manchu territory in the Treaty of Kyakhta. In May, 1858, profiting from the war between China and the Western powers, Russia extorted a confirmation of this annexation and claimed a condominium over the territory east of the Ussuri River, which flows into the Amur from the south. The following year, at a time when European armies were in control of Peking, Russia obtained the outright cession of the land beyond the Ussuri—today the Maritime Territory of Siberia with its capital at the seaport of Vladivostok.

Russia's presence in these far places did not have any great impact on the Chinese people. The present Chinese Communist government, however, has used the story of the Amur lands and the Maritime Territory to reproach the "revisionist" Soviet Union for profiting from the spoliations of the imperialist czars and for making no show of repentance or compensation. The Western "imperialists" have abandoned all their concessions, rights, and privileges, say the Chinese Communists—choosing for the sake of *this* argument to ignore Britain's continued foothold in Hong Kong. It is a good point for polemics, but hardly a serious issue of policy, although open hostilities between the Chinese and the Russians did break out along the banks of the Ussuri in 1969.

The years between the death of the Emperor Hsien Fêng in 1861 and the death of his successor, T'ung Chih, in 1875 are known in Chinese history as the T'ung Chih Restoration. It is not a "restoration" in the Western sense, but rather a "revival," and it has been characterized by a modern historian as the last rally of the old order in China, the last attempt to modernize and, at the same time, to save the empire. A regency under the Empress Dowager Tz'ŭ Hsi, an ignorant but forceful woman, dominated the court. Her influence was reactionary, unlike that of the contemporary ruler of Japan, who was to effect a rapid modernization that would bring Japan to economic and military equality with the West.

Li Hung-chang and the other great Chinese viceroys who had crushed the T'ai P'ings ruled in the provinces. They attempted a cautious modernization; no coherent plan of national development was undertaken. The reformers hardly dared to affront popular superstition by building railways; they would have disrupted the graves of ancestors. They did not care to exploit mineral resources; this would have disturbed the earth gods, aroused popular ire, and, furthermore, required large capital expenditure. But the great viceroys were interested in strengthening the country's

As a result of the Boxer Rebellion, foreign troops (opposite) marched into Peking. The Boxers proved to be no match for the foreigners. At right, captured rebels are kept under surveillance by their captors, members of the United States Sixth Cavalry (at rear).

defenses. Arsenals were built; a modern navy was constructed, and the army was equipped with modern arms instead of swords and bows. Steamships were purchased. However, ships have to be commanded by trained men: young naval officers were therefore selected to be sent abroad to Britain, then the obvious place to learn the naval arts.

Sending students abroad brought about unintended consequences. Among the young naval cadets sent to serve in the British navy was Yen Fu, who had entered the new naval academy at Fu-chou at the age of fourteen. Yen Fu spent from 1877 to 1879 in England. He then returned to China, but although he nominally belonged to the naval service, for many years thereafter he devoted his time to other activities inspired by his years in England. Yen Fu realized that it was not merely weapons that had made the Western powers so strong; it was their institutions, and even their political philosophy. According to Yen Fu, wealth and power were the objectives that China must seek if it was to recover or even to survive. He devoted his life to translating into elegant Chinese the works of those English and French writers whom he considered the best exponents of the ideas that had made the West strong. Educated Chinese could now study the secular thought of the West. The invasion and the losses of ports and sovereign rights had done part of the job of awakening the Chinese to Western power, but the introduction of Western thought by Yen Fu, and by others in later years, was to be far more important. A whole generation that doubted the efficacy and relevance of traditional Confucian teaching came to maturity. These men were not attracted by Christianity, but they were, as a rule, captivated by the ideas of democracy and science, and by the liberal philosophy that then dominated the European mind.

Throughout China the barriers were crumbling, but at the court modern ideas were totally ignored. The alienation between rulers and people grew wider as the century wore on. The empress dowager remained entirely unaffected by changes beyond the palace walls. When her weak and dissolute son T'ung Chih died, she enthroned her own nephew, the previous emperor's cousin of the same generation; in so doing she violated the laws of succession, which required that the new emperor be an heir of the generation after that of the deceased monarch. Not only was the new emperor, Kuang Hsü, her sister's son, but he was just four years old. Another long regency was secured for the empress dowager.

Under her rule China suffered further losses of territory and prestige. War with France (1882–1885) led, in spite of some Chinese military successes, to the loss of suzerainty over Vietnam, then known as Annam. War with Japan (1894–1895) led to the expulsion of Chinese influence from Taiwan and Korea, and brought foreign intrusions into Manchuria, first Japanese and then Russian. The idea of partitioning the Chinese empire grew in the minds of Western statesmen and their constituencies. Spheres of influence were proclaimed to prevent rivalries between the future colonial masters, who marked out in advance their shares of the dying empire. Britain was to lord it in the Yangtze valley and the Canton area. France would have southwest China, adjoining its newly acquired possessions in Vietnam. Russia would have the northeast; Germany was to claim Shantung province for its share; and even Belgium and other small European powers expected, by means of railway development, to dominate wide regions, which they could hardly hope to annex outright. Japan, the apt pupil of the Western imperialists, had its own ambitions, and these were becoming the most far-reaching of all.

Foreign pressures produced two successive reactions from the Chinese. The first led to the Hundred Days of Reform, initiated by the educated younger generation of officials. In 1898 a young official of great intellectual ability, a Cantonese named K'ang Yu-wei, managed to gain the confidence of the Emperor Kuang Hsü, who was now of age and was, in name at least, in charge of the government. Actually the emperor was still very much restricted by the authority of his reactionary aunt, the Empress Dowager Tz'ŭ Hsi, whose retirement was only nominal. Kuang Hsü was intelligent and well meaning, and gave ear to K'ang Yu-wei and his associates. Realizing that only drastic and immediate reform could save the dynasty and the country, he inaugurated a policy of sweeping reforms. Not much could be done. Some of the reforms were overdue and much needed, and many were of secondary significance; but all aroused the anger and fear of the reactionary forces.

The program of reform was to appear mild, conservative, and inadequate a few years later, when all its proposals were adopted as a matter of course. But the empress dowager and her supporters were determined to stop the reforms. Kuang Hsü was betrayed by the General Yüan Shih-k'ai, in whom he had put his trust; he was seized and confined for the rest of his life to an island apartment on the palace lake. The empress dowager resumed control of the government, executed the reformers she could catch, and abolished all the reforms except one, the newly created imperial university, the dynamic center of modern thinking in China and perhaps the most potent intellectual institution in all Asia.

Soon there was another reaction to foreign pressures: the popular uprising called the Boxer Rebellion. It began in Shantung, where the rather warlike inhabitants, who were suffering from the effects of disastrous floods and famine, were roused by the highhanded methods of the new German authorities in the leased port of Ch'ing-tao and in the territory lying along the line of the German-built railway. The Boxers were at first anti-Manchu, but they soon swung their power behind the dynasty in a fierce, blind wave of xenophobia, which embraced not only all foreigners but also all Chinese who had in any way adopted foreign customs. Admitted to Peking by the court, the Boxers murdered the German minister and then in the year 1900 laid siege to the foreign legations. An international expedition of the Western powers, including the United States, came to relieve the legations. The foreigners captured Peking and wrung from the fugitive court a treaty, which deprived China of still more rights, reducing its sovereignty to what the present rulers would call a semicolonial status. It was a ruinous development for the dynasty, which survived for only ten more years, "more or less" as a hostage.

During the first decade of the twentieth century the republican revolutionary movement developed rapidly, gathering impetus from the chaotic state of the country. After the deaths of the Emperor Kuang Hsü and the empress dowager in 1908, no competent successor appeared to wield the powers of the throne. In 1911 revolution broke out, and early in 1912 the dynasty abdicated. The Chinese revolution appeared to have triumphed. Events were to show that it had a tortuous course to follow. The utopia that the ardent young republicans believed would arise overnight did not materialize; the fall of the Manchus was only the first step on a very long journey that has not yet ended. Yet a decisive step had been taken; the bastions of the old Chinese world were breached forever. No matter what line the revolution would take, it would not restore the monarchy, the Confucian educational system, or the old society.

355

East and West

One of the earliest accurate descriptions of China ever circulated in the West was written around A.D. 630 by Theophylact Simocatta, a Byzantine chronicler. Although it was based exclusively on secondhand information, Theophylact's work remained one of the most trustworthy sources of knowledge about China until the transcription of Marco Polo's remarkable travel journals late in the thirteenth century. Polo's account was firsthand, and it was on the whole quite accurate, although he did embellish it occasionally with fanciful details, such as a description of a palace "all covered with gold and silver" and an account of "twelve thousand bridges of stone" in Hang-chou.

Jesuit missionaries, led by the intrepid Matteo Ricci, brought the Christian evangel to the Chinese capital by 1601, and soon began writing home about China in glowing terms. Their benign dispatches were made even more benign by editors before their publication. The result was that a highly idealized portrait of China spread throughout Europe. It held enormous appeal for seventeenth- and eighteenth-century Europeans, who were searching for an ideal of enlightenment on which to base their own societies. The philosopher Leibnitz wished for "the Chinese to send missionaries to us," and Voltaire declared that the Chinese empire was "the most excellent the world has ever seen."

Europe's infatuation with the Orient was short-lived. In the late eighteenth century the West's rapid technical and intellectual advances convinced Europeans of their own superiority. The publication of journals, kept by the merchants who traded with the Chinese, revealed the seamier side of Chinese life. Cries for civil service reforms based on the Chinese model were heard in England as late as 1840, but the "cult of China" was moribund. The philosopher Hegel summed up Europe's view—or misconception—of China when he said, "the history of China has shown no development . . . we cannot concern ourselves with it any further."

An engraving from an eighteenth-century French history depicts the birth of Confucius. The scene, which is strongly reminiscent of a Christian nativity tableau, includes a group of celestial musicians, who celebrate the sage's arrival.

THE IMAGE OF CHINA

The myth of the homogeneous Confucian state—stable, benevolently despotic, and enduring—was wholeheartedly endorsed and promoted by such eminent eighteenth-century Europeans as Voltaire and Montesquieu. Oliver Goldsmith lauded China's supposed immutability in *The Citizen of the World*, declaring that the land had experienced "but one revolution of any continuance in the space of four thousand years," a fact that led the author to "despise all other nations on the comparison." But it was Chinese goods, not Chinese ideas, that had the greater impact on eighteenth-century Europe. At the height of the craze for *chinoiserie*, Frederick II of Hesse-Cassel built an entire Chinese village, and less-extravagant Europeans furnished their homes with silk wall hangings, lacquered furniture, and delicate tea services.

This rococo showplace, designed for a Roman celebration of Chinese culture in 1772, *was a by-product of Europe's enthusiasm for* chinoiserie. *The contemporary painting opposite was done in China, although it is European in style; it shows a Western lady with Oriental features sitting in an elegant drawing room as a servant brings in tea.*

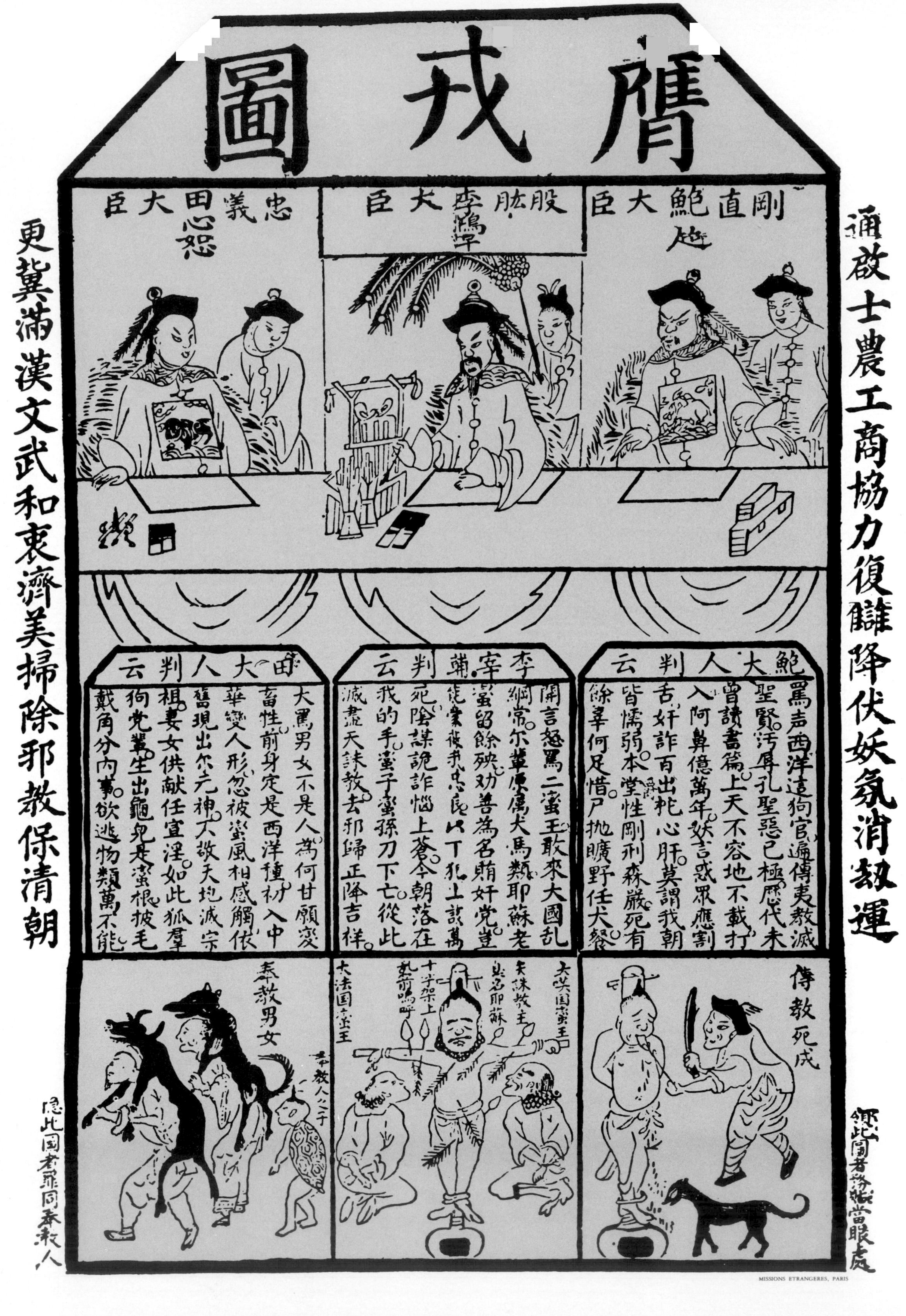

膺戒圖

忠義田心怒 大臣　**股肱李鴻章 大臣**　**剛直鮑超 大臣**

右欄（右邊豎行）：通啟士農工商協力復讎降伏妖氣消殺運

左欄（左邊豎行）：更冀滿漢文武和衷濟美掃除邪教保清朝

右下小字：懸此圖者務張當眼處

左下小字：隱此圖者飛同奉教人

田大人判云

大罵男女不是人為何甘願變畜牲前身定是西洋種初入中華變人形忽被蜜風相感觸依舊現出爾元神大敬天地滅宗祖妻女供獻任宣淫如此狐群披毛戴角分內事欲逃物類萬不能

李宰輔判云

開言怒罵二蜜王散來大國亂我綱常爾輩原屬犬馬類耶蘇老死陰謀說詐惱上蒼死的手蜜子蜜孫刀下亡從此滅盡天誅教去邪歸正降吉祥

鮑大人判云

大罵聲西洋遠狗官遍傳夷教滅聖賢污辱孔聖惡已極歷代未曾讀書篇上天不容地不載打入阿鼻億萬年妖言惑眾應割舌奸詐百出粍心肝莫謂我朝無刑森嚴死有皆儒弱本堂性剛除草何足惜尸拋曠野任犬餐

奉教男女　**奉教人之子**

大法國十蜜王　**大英國蜜王**　**天誅教主**　**耶蘇名吔**　**十字架上蜜王**

傳教死戒

IGNORANCE AND ISOLATION

The idealized conception of China that had been popularized by Voltaire and others was supplanted by an equally inaccurate and considerably less laudatory view. China's "eternal standstill" was disparaged, not admired, by European critics, many of whom felt that Confucianism had dramatically retarded the process of modernization in China. Baffled by the country's incomprehensible isolationism and spurred by hopes of securing additional trade concessions, the major powers opened China by force. The foreigners confined themselves to their comfortable compounds; they were fearful of the natives, whose language few Europeans spoke and whose customs fewer understood. Mutual ignorance led to a series of diplomatic crises and punitive military actions, which eventually culminated in the bloody Boxer Rebellion.

A. DIOSY, *The New Far East*, NEW YORK, 1898

Conceived by Kaiser Wilhelm and executed by the German artist Hermann Knackfuss, this work of art was intended to act as a clarion call to European chauvinism. Entitled The Yellow Peril, *it pictures "Germany" urging the countries of Europe to unite against the distant threat of China—five years before the outbreak of the Boxer Rebellion. The Chinese poster opposite depicts three officials (top) with anti-Christian quotations attributed to them. Below, at left, is a Christian family, "unfit to belong to the human species" and clad in animal skins; at center appears "Jesus the old barbarian . . . the cause of all calamities." At right, a missionary's tongue is being cut out.*

WESTERN
IMPERIALISM

During the nineteenth century, China was semicolonized by not one, but half a dozen foreign powers. As a result, the country was exposed to endless profiteering and denied the slim benefits normally associated with colonial status (such as protection against attacks by other predators). China was not so much colonized as cannibalized by the foreign powers, who were determined to stake out huge and hugely profitable spheres of influence for themselves—at gunpoint, if necessary. An 1857 blockade of Canton forced the Chinese to open eleven new Treaty Ports to foreign trade; the seizure of Peking three years later resulted in the establishment of permanent foreign legations in the capital. By 1898 thirteen of China's eighteen provinces had become foreign spheres of influence.

Dominated and exploited by foreigners, China was ripe for the apparently spontaneous and intensely xenophobic Boxer Rebellion that erupted in 1900. The uprising was quickly quelled, but fear of similar insurrections, coupled with ignorance of the real causes of the rebellion, inspired Westerners to condemn China as roundly as they had once praised it. Expressing the new view, an American journal editorialized: "China is self-centered . . . arrogant, hostile to other lands and peoples. It has always been so."

In this turn-of-the-century American cartoon the Western trading powers—and Japan—gather to dismember China after the Boxer Rebellion.

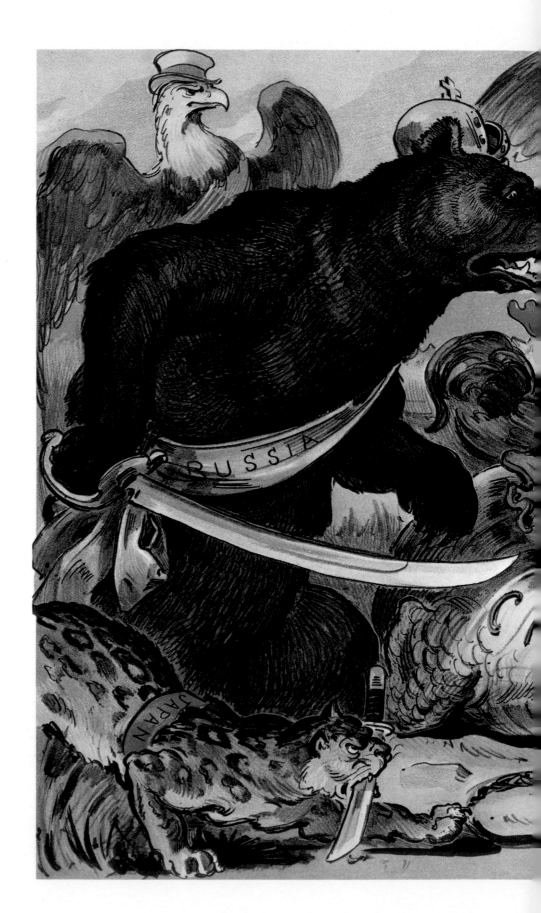

14 Modern China
(1912 *to the present*)

Two leaders of the Chinese revolution, Sun Yat-sen (seated) and his protégé, Chiang Kai-shek, are seen in a photograph that was taken around the year 1924.

The revolution of 1911, which brought about the fall of the Chinese empire in the following year, was the result of a long and growing agitation for change; but the actual outbreak of the uprising was accidental. For more than fifteen years Dr. Sun Yat-sen, an overseas Chinese who had abandoned a career in medicine to become a revolutionary, had plotted and planned revolution from Hong Kong, Tokyo, and Singapore, interspersing his activities with fund-raising tours in the United States, Europe, and southeast Asia—wherever there were overseas Chinese communities large enough to make worthwhile contributions. Revolts in China had become frequent, but they had always failed. They had been mainly directed toward the capture of the city of Canton. Most of the first revolutionaries were from the Canton region, and they seem to have had little contact with dissidents in other parts of the country. However, as large numbers of Chinese from the wealthy Yangtze provinces brought back new ideas from foreign universities, revolutionary doctrine took root in central China.

In the early years of the twentieth century, after the Boxer Rebellion, the prestige of the dynasty sank very low. Revolutionary ideas spread among the young officers of the "modern" army, which was being formed to replace the archaic force that had so obviously failed to defend the country in 1900. It was the army officers rather than the professional revolutionaries who proved to be the decisive forces in the outbreak of the revolution. Later the officers were to dominate the political life of the republic that arose as a result of their actions.

On the evening of October 10, 1911, an explosion occurred in a house in the Russian concession at Han-k'ou, a Treaty Port situated on the Yangtze in the center of China. The police investigated and found that the house was a revolutionary headquarters and an arsenal, where grenades were being made. They also found a list of the members of an illegal revolutionary party. This list contained the names of many army officers stationed nearby. Alerted to their danger, the officers did not hesitate to act. That same night they roused their commander, General Li Yüan-hung, and, it is reported, gave him the choice of dying or assuming the leadership of the revolt. Li chose life. He had had no connection with the revolutionary movement. But as a result of his help, the important triple cities of Wu-han— Han-k'ou, Han-yang and Wu-ch'ang—were taken over without a shot being fired. All political prisoners were released and officials loyal to the dynasty fled.

The defection of the army revealed that the dynasty had totally lost esteem and loyalty. No civil revolutionary had had a hand in the uprising. At the time Sun Yat-sen was in the United States, and he read about the revolt in a Denver newspaper. Sun's deputy, Huang Hsing, was also overseas, but he was closer to home. When he learned what had happened, he hurried back to take command of the revolution. The seizure of Wu-han, one of the most important urban areas in all China, was a tremendous moral victory for the revolutionaries. Only a few months earlier one of Sun's many efforts to take Canton had failed. The results of the Wu-han revolt were astonishing: throughout south China one province after another joined the revolution. In most cases there was no imperial resistance; very often the viceroys and governors themselves headed the revolutionary movement. Within weeks all south China was lost to the dynasty.

In the north and west the situation was different at first; but the revolution eventually spread to these regions too. Its spread was marked by violence. In Ch'eng-tu, capital of Ssŭch'uan province, the Manchu viceroy was killed and there were large-scale disorders. At Sian in Shensi the garrison of Manchu Bannermen was massacred; Moslems rescued pretty Manchu girls and young children, to be brought up as members of their community. In the north and west the movement was spearheaded not only by the army but by a secret anti-Manchu society. This was the Ko Lao Hui, or Society of the Elder Brethren, which permeated all manner of organizations, including the army.

The dynasty, in desperate straits, eventually turned for help to the leading general in the imperial service, Yüan Shih-k'ai. Yüan alone might have induced the northern troops to fight against the rebels. He had suppressed the Boxers in his province; before that he had turned traitor on behalf of the reactionary Empress Dowager Tz'ŭ Hsi, betraying her nephew, the Emperor Kuang Hsü. For this he had been dismissed from his post after the death of Tz'ŭ Hsi by Kuang Hsü's brother, who succeeded to power. Now the dynasty depended on Yüan; and Yüan bargained. He would assume command, he said, only if he were also appointed to the office of prime minister with full powers. The Manchus had to agree. Yüan sent his troops south and recaptured Han-k'ou and Han-yang, but he did not attempt to cross the Yangtze to take Wu-ch'ang. Having demonstrated the army's strength and its loyalty to him, he started negotiating secretly with the republicans. His negotiations were designed to end the civil war by forcing the abdication of the dynasty and to secure the future predominance of Yüan Shih-k'ai.

Yüan's plans were well laid. He was favored by the foreign powers, who saw him as a "strong man" who had put down the Boxers in Shantung; they felt he could be relied upon to maintain order and safeguard foreign trade and investment. As a result, his plans came to fruition. Yüan and the republicans joined forces. Sun Yat-sen returned to China in tri-

Yüan Shih-k'ai (above, right), a Manchu official, was given the task of suppressing the 1911 revolution. Yüan managed to seize control of the revolution and tried, without success, to make himself emperor. In the 1920's the forces of Chinese nationalism were reorganized by Russian agents, who tried to integrate the Kuomintang and the Communists. One such agent, Mikhail Borodin, is shown above with an interpreter. Opposite is a modern Communist painting portraying the young Mao Tsetung looming over China's landscape.

umph, landing at Shanghai on Christmas Day. He was installed as provisional president in Nanking, which was proclaimed the new capital. On February 12, 1912, the Manchu dynasty, bowing to the inevitable, ended its two hundred sixty-eight years of rule and formally established the republic by imperial decree. The Manchus surrendered imperial power and accepted the Favorable Treatment Agreement, by which the infant emperor retained his title, his court, a large pension, and possession of the Forbidden City and the summer palace.

On the day following the abdication, Sun Yat-sen resigned the office of provisional president, and Yüan was unanimously elected in his place. Yüan was elected on the condition that he come to Nanking and govern from the new capital; but he did not want to leave Peking. In order to avoid the move he permitted, and even encouraged, his troops in Peking to mutiny and burn down a part of the city close, but not too close, to the foreign legation quarter. He then claimed that the troops could not be restrained if he were to leave the north. The frightened foreign diplomats, with clear and recent memories of the Boxer Rebellion, supported him. Yüan and the government remained in Peking.

The republicans' plans called for the election of a parliament to decide on a permanent constitution. The man most able to organize its work was Sung Chiao-jen, a devoted and liberal democrat. The election returned a large majority for the revolutionary republican party; it was clear that the republicans would dominate parliament. This did not suit Yüan. Sung Chiao-jen was assassinated while he was on his way to the Shanghai railway station at Peking. Subsequent inquiries established without doubt that this act was inspired and ordered by Yüan Shih-k'ai. The republican party was left intimidated and leaderless. The open corruption of the election, and the republi-

cans' subsequent concern with voting themselves large salaries, did not add to their prestige. The Chinese people had had no experience with democratic government. A vote was seen as a commodity for which money would be paid. The price of votes was quoted on the exchange.

Yüan's next step was to negotiate a very large "reorganization loan" from foreign banks. He did this without consulting the parliament—a move that was, of course, unconstitutional. A great outcry arose from the republicans. Yüan countered by dismissing many military commanders who were likely to be loyal to the republic and by sending his own followers to take their commands. The movement to organize a revolt against Yüan proved to be a failure. The opposition collapsed and Sun Yat-sen fled to Japan. One of Yüan's more notorious reactionary generals, Chang Hsün, took Nanking and allowed his troops to sack that ill-starred city. This occurred in June, 1913. On October 6 Yüan surrounded the parliament building with a villainous mob that refused to disperse or to permit any food to be brought in until the hungry members elected Yüan president. Parliament having served its turn, Yüan proscribed the majority party (now called the Kuomintang, or Nationalist party), accusing it of having been implicated in revolt. The parliament, deprived of a quorum, was then dissolved. Throughout 1914 and 1915 Yüan steadily moved toward what was soon recognized as his goal: his own elevation to the throne. A picked consultative assembly advocated a new dynasty with Yüan as emperor. Yüan made the ritual refusals, but accepted the offer. In December, 1915, it was announced that the new dynasty would be proclaimed on the first of January, 1916.

Yüan's moves seemed effective, but there were a number of factors that were unfavorable

Mao Tse-tung

to him. The first World War had broken out, and although China was still neutral, divisions among the European powers created great dangers for the country. However, the most obvious danger came from Japan, which now enjoyed a free hand in China, and Japan did not like Yüan Shih-k'ai. Many years earlier he had for a time successfully opposed Japan in Korea; his new monarchy seemed to promise a stability that would block Japanese ambitions in China. In January, 1915, Japan secretly submitted to Yüan the Twenty-One Demands, which have become infamous in Chinese history. Had they all been accepted, China would have become, in effect, a Japanese protectorate, with the Japanese supervising the army and police. Yüan tried to temporize and leaked the news of the Japanese demands to the Western press. He had to accept some of the demands, but with the support of foreign powers fearful of Japanese predominance, he was able to refuse the more far-reaching ones. His prestige was dealt a serious blow, however, and Japan was able to continue exerting pressure on China.

As soon as the intention of proclaiming a new monarchy was announced, opposition began to appear from an unlikely quarter, from Yüan's own following. As generals in a republic, they held key positions. They did not relish the prospect that a stable and consolidated monarchy might diminish their influence and power. Yüan was old and would soon die; his son was an arrogant and foolish youth toward whom they felt no loyalty. The Japanese were soon financing a revolt against Yüan. On Christmas Day, 1915, the military governor of Yünnan rebelled against the emperor-elect. The date of the revolt proved convenient; it later permitted the Chinese world to observe December 25 as a holiday—but as a republican festival rather than as a Christian one.

Yüan at first regarded the revolt as of no

Shanghai's international settlement (above), known as the Bund, was the symbol of foreign control over China and a target of Nationalist hatred.

importance; but it soon became evident to him that the revolt was spreading. In the west governor after governor came over to the revolutionary cause; the troops sent against the rebels joined their forces. At last the most trusted northern commanders sent a petition to Yüan, urging him to renounce the throne. Yüan had to recognize that his cause was all but lost. He announced his intention to continue as president and postponed the establishment of the monarchy. However, this did not satisfy his enemies, and they continued to oppose him. On June 6, 1916, the would-be emperor, who had been in failing health for some time, died—of "eating bitterness," as the Chinese people put it.

Yüan's diverse opponents had neither common tactics nor unity of purpose. In July, 1917, there was an abortive attempt to put the Manchu dynasty back on the throne. The move was supported solely by the reactionary General Chang Hsün and proved only how dead any loyalty to the dynasty really was. The southern revolutionaries tried to restore the parliamentary republic; the northern militarists had no

intention of yielding power to such men, and they placed one of their own number in the presidential chair. Before long, the northern generals were fighting each other and the southern forces for control of Peking and of the revenues that accrued to the government. These revenues were largely derived from customs collection, which was controlled by the foreign-staffed Maritime Customs service, and from the salt monopoly, which was also foreign run. The warlord era had begun.

It was to last about ten years, from 1916 to 1925. In this dismal epoch the fabric of the Chinese state all but collapsed. The central government dissolved, and wars between rival warlords swept the country. Few combatants were killed, but the countryside was pillaged as landlords fled to the safety of large cities and their bailiffs bargained with bandits and militarists for a share of the exorbitant rents.

One of the most significant casualties of the warlord era, unremarked at the time, was the democratic ideal of the early republican revolutionaries. Bargaining with untrustworthy warlords, Sun Yat-sen tried to maintain a "legal" republican government in Canton; but several times he was driven into exile in the foreign concessions at Shanghai. In Peking puppet governments, installed by the warlord who was locally dominant at the moment, went through the motions of ruling China and were accepted by the foreign powers as the legitimate government. Their duration was usually less than one year. Reunification was the hope of all, but reunification by whom? By some ruthless and corrupt warlord, or by the ineffectual southern republicans, or, as some began to fear, by foreign conquerors? Japan was well satisfied with the collapse of China.

The Chinese people themselves began to react against this demoralizing spectacle. On May 4, 1919, the students of Peking National University rioted to protest against the venal government that had accepted Japan's acquisition of the former German-leased naval base of Ch'ing-tao. This had come about by a decision of the Versailles Peace Conference, implementing a secret agreement concluded during the war without the knowledge of the Chinese government. Students burned motorcars and houses belonging to the corrupt politicians. The Chinese delegation at Versailles, encouraged by these protests, refused to sign the Versailles Treaty. (May 4 was a landmark in the development of the Chinese revolution and is celebrated as such by the Communist regime.) In May, 1925, a student protest against the suppression of a textile workers' strike in Shanghai led to another shooting affray, in which the International Settlement police killed eleven students. This sparked off furious nationwide antiforeign resentment. The event was used for their own purposes both by Nationalist opponents of the spineless Peking regime and by the nascent Communist movement. The Communists organized boycott pickets and brought British and Japanese trade with China to a standstill.

These movements were used by the new political forces, but not created by them; the Chinese revolution cannot be understood in terms of a conspiracy. The rising frustration and despair of an ill-governed people was its real driving force.

Another development of the warlord era that went unnoticed was the growth of the Chinese Communist party. In 1921 thirteen men, including Mao Tse-tung, met to form this party; at the same time a branch of the

The alliance between the Communists and the Kuomintang ruptured shortly after a Communist-led mob (above) seized the British concession in Hank'ou in 1927. That year Communists also rose in Canton. Chiang's forces quelled their revolt and executed numerous rebels (top), who were easily identifiable because their skin was stained red by the dye from red scarves that they had worn during the revolt.

THE HOOVER INSTITUTION, HUSTON COLLECTION

UNITED PRESS INTERNATIONAL

party was formed by Chinese students in Paris, one of the students being Chou En-lai. Legend would make Mao the founder of the party, but in fact he was one of the least important members present at its establishment. The new party, very much under the tutelage of the Russian-controlled Comintern, soon made an agreement with Sun Yat-sen, who was still leader of the Nationalist movement. According to the compact, members of the Communist party might join the Kuomintang as individuals, but not en bloc. At the same time Sun, once more in power in Canton, accepted Russian military and political aid to strengthen his regime and reorganize his party. Appeals for such aid to the Western powers had been turned down; they continued to recognize the ephemeral regimes in Peking.

Sun Yat-sen died in March, 1925, a few weeks before the shooting of the students in Shanghai plunged the whole of China into xenophobia. But his regime in Canton was strengthened by the antiforeign movement, and it survived the loss of its leader. Very soon Sun's Nationalists were reorganized by Russian experts, rearmed, and prepared to take the field against the local warlords. These were defeated, and the Nationalists embarked on a great campaign to overthrow the more powerful northern warlords and reunify China. This "Northern Expedition," as it was called, was launched late in 1926 and met with immediate and sweeping success. The warlords were driven from the southern provinces and from Wu-han; then Nanking fell, and the armies of the new revolution approached Shanghai. The Communist party, aided by its boycott pickets, rose in the Chinese area of the city and seized it from the troops of the local warlord on March 22, 1927.

The troops of the Treaty Powers waited in the foreign concessions of Shanghai. It seemed as if war between the Treaty Powers and the

Deprived of salt and other basic commodities by a Kuomintang blockade, the Communists were forced to abandon their Kiangsi province stronghold in 1934. Nearly 100,000 Communist soldiers broke out of encirclement and began a year-long march to Shensi province in the north. A modern Communist painting (below) shows one episode of the march, the perilous crossing of the Ta-tu River.

In 1937 Chinese soldiers, massing to counter a Japanese invasion of the northeast provinces, marched to the battle front along the ancient Great Wall.

ton to Wu-han, of being under their influence. The Wu-han government was also under the influence of Nationalist party men who were personally opposed to Chiang. On April 12, 1927, Chiang struck at the Communist movement in Shanghai, massacring all Communists he could catch. Chou En-lai, who had played a large role in organizing the Communist seizure of Shanghai, escaped the slaughter by good fortune and by the quickness of his wit. Similar purges were carried out in Canton and in Nanking. In the latter city on April 18 Chiang set up a new Nationalist government in opposition to the hitherto "legal" Nationalist government in Wu-han. The Communists were excluded from Chiang's government. In July, 1927, the Wu-han government, itself turning against the Communists, expelled its Russian advisers and united with Chiang's regime in Nanking. Chiang's temporary retirement facilitated this unification and saved face for the Wu-han leaders, who were in fact yielding to him.

These divisions had delayed the campaign to eliminate the last warlord of importance, Chang Tso-lin. Chang controlled all north China and, in so far as the Japanese permitted it, Manchuria. In April, 1928, the Nationalist advance was resumed; Chiang's troops swept into Peking in June. Chang Tso-lin had withdrawn to Manchuria. As Chang's train approached Mukden, at a point where the Chinese line from Peking crossed the tracks of the Japanese-controlled South Manchurian Railway, the train was blown up by a bomb and Chang was killed. No one in China seriously doubted who was responsible. The Japanese were worried that Chang Tso-lin might become infected with the Nationalist sentiment that was now dominant throughout China.

The warlord era was basically at an end; the new Nationalist government in Nanking was in power over most of China and was reluc-

Chinese revolutionary forces was almost inevitable. But Chiang Kai-shek, who was the commander in chief of the combined revolutionary armies, did not think so. He was in touch with old associates in Shanghai—bankers, merchants, and others, including the leaders of the secret societies who controlled much of Shanghai's labor. These men did not want a Communist revolution or a foreign invasion. They were Nationalists and, as the modern Chinese would put it, members of the bourgeois class.

Chiang was also opposed to the Communists and suspected the Nationalist government, which had been transferred from Can-

In August, 1937, a month after the Japanese launched their undeclared war on China, Shanghai was attacked. Below, an ambulance crew helps the wounded.

tantly recognized by the Treaty Powers. Their diplomats had now to leave Peking, a pleasant and gracious city, to dwell in the hot, humid, and rather run-down Nanking. Nanking had once been a glorious city, but that had been more than a thousand years earlier. Still, it was less than two hundred miles from Shanghai. This may have been some compensation to the foreign residents, but it proved to be deleterious to the Chinese government.

Shanghai, with its foreign concessions, was the only really important center of modern industry, finance, and commerce in China. It was gay and entertaining, open to foreign influences, and permissive in its attitudes. It was nicknamed the "Paris of the East," which may be a slur on Paris. It was highly attractive to the officials and politicians of the Nationalist regime. They could maintain apartments or homes in Shanghai and commute to Nanking by a fast and efficient nightly express train

equipped with sleeping cars. One did not really need to live in Nanking at all. This way of life might be somewhat expensive, but the money for it could be found by any wide-awake official or politician.

The new regime in Nanking was corrupted in more ways than one by its proximity to Shanghai. It came under the domination of the wealthy businessmen of Shanghai. Men who had never lived in, or often so much as visited, the Chinese countryside were now the elite of China, sharing power with the army. Chiang represented the army; his in-laws—the Soong family—the money of Shanghai. These two forces dominated the Nationalist regime. There was no significant power to speak for the peasants or defend their interests.

The Communist party took up that role, and thereby secured its power base in China. On August 1, 1927, after the purge at Shanghai and the expulsion of the Communists from

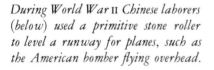

During World War II Chinese laborers (below) used a primitive stone roller to level a runway for planes, such as the American bomber flying overhead.

Wu-han, units of the revolutionary army, commanded by officers of Communist allegiance, mutinied at Nan-ch'ang in Kiangsi and seized the city. Five days later they were forced to withdraw in the face of superior power. The incident, now recognized as a landmark in the course of the Chinese revolution, was considered trifling at the time, and the troops were forgotten by the world. Their leader was Chu Teh, and Lin Piao was one of his officers. The revolutionary army moved south and tried, without success, to take and hold various southern cities. In the spring of the next year the army joined up with another refugee Communist group in Hunan province at the remote mountain stronghold of Chingkang Shan. The leader of that group was Mao Tsetung. The famous Mao-Chu combination was formed; and in due course it was to lead the Communist party to total victory.

From the first the refugees began to eliminate landlords, dividing the land and gaining the goodwill of the peasants in the territory under their control. This policy was not sanctioned, and perhaps not really understood, by Moscow and by the clandestine Communist headquarters in Shanghai. But it succeeded where alternatives more in line with orthodox Marxist teaching had failed. The Red Army's dutiful attempts to follow orthodox policy by capturing and holding large cities, such as Ch'ang-sha, were disastrous. The people of the cities, cowed or indifferent, did not rise to join the Communist cause. They were not, in fact, real proletarians thirsting for revolution; there was no industrial working class in China's inland cities at that time, only journeymen, craftsmen, and menial laborers. But the Russians did not believe this. They felt the revolution had to be based on the working class, not on conservative, illiterate, and superstitious peasants. The peasants, however, had had enough of rent-wracking landlords, band-

its, and pillaging government troops; they were in a revolutionary mood and gave full support to the Red Army.

When Chiang Kai-shek realized this, he assumed that a campaign of "bandit extermination" would be required to get rid of the Communist army. But he completely underestimated his opponents. Five unsuccessful campaigns failed to dislodge the Communists from their bases in south China. The Red Army, swollen with recruits and deserters from the Nationalist forces, had grown to 300,000

"The American pilot helped you to chase the Japanese out of the Chinese sky," proclaims the propaganda leaflet shown above, portraying an American crushing a Japanese soldier. Such leaflets were dropped in occupied territories during World War II.

375

After Japan's fall, Chiang Kai-shek (left) and Mao Tse-tung (right) met to discuss the organization of a postwar coalition government. The two were unable to reach a settlement, and civil war soon erupted between their forces.

men. The Communist area in the south, generally known as the Kiangsi Soviet, was proclaimed as the Chinese Soviet Republic.

Chiang followed his plan of "bandit extermination" from October, 1933, till October, 1934, and it finally gave him some sort of solution. The inland province of Kiangsi produces no salt. Deprivation of salt would, in time, undermine the health of the Red Army as well as that of the ordinary inhabitants. A blockade could also prevent other essential supplies from reaching the Communists. After a year, the blockade was so successful that the Communist army had to break out of Kiangsi or be forced into surrender. The army's escape from Kiangsi, and its Long March to refuge in distant Shensi province, was made possible by the fact that the southern and southwestern perimeters of the Communist area were blockaded by provincial troops who were of poorer quality than Chiang's regulars and who may have had little enthusiasm for his cause. When attacked they preferred to give way.

The Communist army and all of its followers who were deemed strong enough to march, about 100,000 men and perhaps 50,000 dependents, broke out of encirclement; but they did not march north as expected. They struck south and west through the inland provinces of Hunan, Kueichou, Ssŭch'uan, and Ch'inghai. Ultimately they traveled through Kansu to north Shensi. The distance covered, with many detours, was about 6,000 miles, and the march took exactly one year.

In the far west the Communists had to cross the Tibetan grasslands, a very high, desolate region, largely swamp and without inhabitants or roads. They crossed great ranges of snow-clad mountains. They were never really brought to battle or intercepted by the Nationalist forces, who tried to overtake them from the rear. The warlords who still remained in these far-off provinces thought only of

their own security and their own wealth. They concentrated their forces in a few large cities and did not stir forth from them until the Communists had passed by. The countryside was left to the invaders. They treated its inhabitants with careful kindness and scrupulous discipline. All supplies and services were paid for. No looting was tolerated; there was no requisitioning without cash payment. In the provinces through which it passed the Red Army left a fund of goodwill and an almost awe-struck admiration for its discipline, such as no Chinese army had ever before displayed. All this was to prove a great asset for the future.

The Long March was costly; only 20,000 fighting men survived its rigors. At its end, this small force found itself established in a wild mountain zone of the northwestern province of Shensi—a poor and barren region, but one easily defended. The region was inhabited by a sturdy peasantry, who had suffered gross oppressions. It was not long before the Red Army made up its losses from among the local inhabitants.

Meanwhile Chiang had other troubles. In the north, the Japanese had continually encroached on Chinese territory. In 1931 they took over all of Manchuria and set up the puppet empire of Manchukuo, with the former Manchu boy-emperor as its nominal ruler. In 1932 the Japanese attacked the Chinese section of Shanghai from their base in the International Settlement; they encountered very strong resistance and had a long fight to gain even a small area of the city. Chiang became rather unpopular for not giving the defenders of Shanghai more support and for not making the attack a *casus belli*; but he still adhered to his policy of "internal pacification before resistance to external attack." This meant fruitless attempts to crush the Communists while giving way to the Japanese. By the end of

1935 it was becoming obvious that the reactionary forces in control of Japan would not be stopped by appeasement. They feared China's rising military capacity and the growth of Communism, and they believed the time had come to strike.

Chiang persisted with his plans to crush the Red Army. In 1936 he assembled a new force for the task. Some of the troops were Manchurian exiles, driven out by the Japanese. They wanted to fight to recover their homeland and not to fight other Chinese. In December, 1936, Chiang, hearing of disaffection among the troops, went to Sian to instill discipline and raise morale. Almost at once the army mutinied and made him a prisoner. He was told he would be put to death unless he agreed to call off the war against the Communists and fight Japan. Chou En-lai arrived to mediate between the mutineers and his old enemy. Chiang yielded, and an agreement was

drawn up, calling for an end to the civil war and for mutual preparation to resist Japan. The Communists agreed to treat Chiang as the head of the Chinese state and the commander in chief of all its armies. They abolished their republic, but retained jurisdiction over its territory, which they called the Border Area Autonomous District.

The Sian agreement saved Chiang's face—and his life—but it was the Communists who really benefited from it. They conceded forms and titles; they gained security, recognition as a legal party, and freedom to mobilize and organize for the coming war with Japan. They also gained immense prestige and were hailed as patriots who had brought the civil war to an end with generous concessions. They won many new friends in circles that before had feared them, and many young students flocked to their new University of Yenan to receive instruction in Marxism and in guerrilla war-

General George C. Marshall (second from left) went to China in 1946 to try to prevent civil war. Marshall, accompanied by Mao Tse-tung (far right), is seen on an inspection tour of Yenan.

377

fare. They did not have long to wait to put their military learning into practice.

At the first opportunity the Japanese struck what they expected to be a decisive blow. On July 7, 1937, the second World War really began for China with a Japanese attack on a small strategic city near Peking. Within days the Japanese seized Peking and much of north China. Under various pretexts their forces had already occupied much of the region. But as the Japanese tried to move south and west, they encountered obstacles.

In the mountain region, which stretches westward from Peking, the Japanese easily dispersed the regular troops commanded by one of the last of the warlords. Then they began to meet guerrillas who were directed from Communist headquarters in Yenan. The Japanese continued to struggle against the guerrillas for the next eight years—until the war ended in 1945. The invaders could occupy the cities, and partially control the few main roads and the only railway, but they could not pacify the countryside. Their attempts to enroll Chinese puppet troops were useless. These forces continually sold their arms to the guerrillas and supplied them with intelligence information.

The peasants were solidly opposed to the invading foreigners, who treated them with great cruelty and harsh reprisals. "Burn all, kill all, loot all" campaigns were launched by

the Japanese; these campaigns created a wilderness in the countryside and drove the people into the arms of the Communists. Japanese military field reports have revealed how clearly officers on the spot realized what was happening; their representations had little effect upon their superiors in Tokyo and Peking. This pattern of resistance and reprisal spread steadily over north China as the regular Nationalist armies were driven to the west. By the end of the war Hopei, Shantung, Honan, Shansi, Anhui, and north Kiangsu, as well as areas in what is now Inner Mongolia, were under guerrilla control. The whole region is perhaps as large as western Europe; at the time it had a population of about two hundred millions.

In central China the Nationalist forces resisted the Japanese with some success for a year or more. By cutting the Yellow River dikes—a terrible expedient that changed the river's course and resulted in floods—the Nationalists checked the Japanese advance. The devastated area was beginning to become habitable only in 1956, nearly twenty years later. The Japanese attack on Shanghai met with stiff resistance, which held up the invaders for three months. Then, using their unchallenged sea power, the Japanese landed to the north and south of Shanghai, and drove the Chinese back to Nanking. They took that city, sacked it, and massacred its inhabitants.

HSIA TING. REPRINTED BY PERMISSION FROM THE AUGUST 1945 ISSUE OF *Fortune* MAGAZINE

The Nationalist government retired, first to Wu-han and then to Chungking, which was almost unassailable beyond the Yangtze gorges. The Japanese occupied the great cities along the Yangtze below the gorges; they took Canton and all the other major southern ports.

China was isolated except for contact by air and by one highway, the Burma Road, which crossed very difficult mountain country. The Japanese continued to believe that one further advance and the loss of yet another city would induce Chiang to surrender. But Chiang refused to give up. As stubborn in a good cause as he had been in a foolish one, he held out, in the full expectation that Japan would soon quarrel with the Western powers, and above all with America. Then in due time victory would come to China and its new allies. Meanwhile, he did nothing but defend the unassailable approaches to Ssǔch'uan province and wait. While he waited, the Japanese attacked at Pearl Harbor, invaded Burma, and cut the Burma Road. More than a year passed before essential supplies could again be brought in in bulk by an airlift from India.

By the policy of inactive defense the Nationalists abandoned to Communist guerrillas the task of actually fighting the Japanese and of defending the people of the invaded provinces. The Kuomintang lost touch with the occupied provinces, and the Communists won the everlasting support of millions of peasants. Moreover, the Nationalist regime was now located in the least advanced and worst governed part of China, where a particularly outmoded and cruel system of land tenure reduced the peasantry to an unjustified poverty. This situation tended to corrupt the Nationalist regime and its army. Bribery became rampant, along with misappropriation of the soldiers' pay, trade with the enemy-held areas, and little-disguised pillage by the soldiers themselves. A dangerous contrast was presented to the Chinese people: on the one hand, a corrupt regime that seemed unaware of the need for reform and that took no active steps to fight the invader; on the other, a puritanically honest regime that reduced rents and equalized taxation, and moreover, continually and with growing success fought the invader at all points, giving him neither surcease nor rest. Relations between Nationalists and Communists deteriorated to the point where open clashes occurred.

Then, in August, 1945, the end came dramatically and unexpectedly. The atomic bombs induced the Japanese to surrender. The Chinese were faced with deciding who should receive the Japanese surrender and who should occupy and administer the cities and provinces the enemy had held. The problem proved insolu-

The corruption of wartime China and the decadence of its upper class are satirized in the scroll above. At far left, a blindfolded journalist attempts to speak, although an official invitation gags his mouth. Behind him, a limousine slips by a group of refugees; to the right of them, officials quibble over the distribution of food and clothing to two soldiers as rats consume the rice at their feet. At center, a wealthy merchant dickers with a peasant who wishes to sell his coat; a prostitute clinging to the merchant holds her nose to avoid smelling the wounded soldier next to her. At center right, a one-eyed censor scrutinizes the work of a seated author, ignoring the commercialized work of the artist standing alongside them. The student at far right buries his nose in a book, ignoring his professor's starving family.

379

An elderly man wearing a hooded robe searches for his son among the ranks of Kuomintang recruits assembled alongside him. These soldiers were the last troops recruited by Chiang Kai-shek.

ble. An American ambassador, General George C. Marshall, came to China to mediate and avert, if he could, a return to civil war. His efforts lasted for months, but were fruitless. No compromise was acceptable to the two sides now that the menace of Japan was removed. The Communists insisted on control of the areas they had liberated and infiltrated. This meant half of China. They also insisted on safeguards that would enable them to resist any attempt at suppression. The effort to form a coalition government was very unwelcome to Chiang Kai-shek, for it involved concessions that he was unwilling to make. Intellectuals and professional people urged a coalition with genuine democratic elections; Marshall agreed with this program, but the existing conditions made its realization impossible. Nationalists and Communists were not political parties fighting on the hustings; they were armed nations contending for huge territories. General Marshall went home, declaring, in effect, "a plague on both your houses."

By the middle of 1946 civil war was widespread. In 1947 there was a total breakdown of negotiations. Chiang had great superiority in numbers and in equipment. His armies had been largely re-equipped by the United States. Chiang also had an air force; the Communists had none. The Communists' weapons were mainly those captured from the Japanese or produced in small factories in the mountains. Yet in two years the Nationalists lost the war. In 1949 they were driven from the mainland to take refuge in Taiwan.

The reasons for this collapse were inherent in the Chinese situation at the end of World War II. Inflation raged in the Nationalist-controlled areas. No wages retained their value. All tried to buy goods or to obtain illegal silver coins or American currency. Under these conditions corrupt dealings were a necessity of life. The government was incompetent and impenitent. It would neither reform nor act with adequate authority. It made no attempt to meet China's social problems. Its soldiers, dispirited by what they knew their families were suffering, had no will to fight their countrymen. As the knowledge spread of far better conditions in the Communist areas, the morale of the Nationalist armies dwindled. Also, strategic errors made the Nationalist situation worse. An attempt to occupy Manchuria while north and central China were in Communist hands, ended in the total surrender of Chiang's best armies. The end was then certain. The Communists advanced to the Yangtze and early in 1949 crossed that river and took Nanking and then Shanghai. South China was occupied with very little fighting in the summer of 1949; then the western provinces surrendered. On October 1, 1949, the People's Republic of China was proclaimed in Peking.

In the last days of the Nationalist regime there had been an attempt to settle the war by negotiation; these negotiations would have brought about, in effect, a slightly disguised Nationalist surrender. Had they been brought to a successful conclusion, the new government would have come to power as the legal successor of the old one. There would have been no questions about diplomatic recognition of the People's Republic or of its membership in the United Nations. The negotiations—which would have saved the world many problems that are still unsolved—were frustrated by Chiang Kai-shek. As a result, many foreign powers, including the United States, do not recognize China, and the Nationalist delegate from Taiwan occupies China's seat at the United Nations. Peking is unrepresented. Although China had suffered terribly from the Japanese invasion, it was not invited to sign the San Francisco Peace Treaty with Japan, and therefore it has never received a penny of reparations. These factors underlie much of the intransigent attitude that the new China assumes in international relations. China is a country with a sense of great grievances unredressed.

Within a year or so of the proclamation of the People's Republic, China was involved in the Korean War. Soldiers, who were called volunteers in order to avoid the disadvantages of openly acknowledged intervention, crossed into Korea in October, 1950, and helped to save the North Korean regime from collapse. The Chinese then advanced to south of Seoul; later they were driven back to the line that now divides North and South Korea. There, after long and tedious negotiations, an armistice was arranged. The Korean War had important consequences for China. It greatly strengthened the prestige of the new regime and increased its acceptance by the Chinese. It also once again brought China into full control of Manchuria. After World War II, Stalin had claimed and obtained the special privileges in Manchuria that czarist Russia had once exercised and that Japan had later inherited: partial control of the railway across northern Manchuria, a naval base at Port Arthur, and special commercial privileges at nearby Dairen, Manchuria's main port. After China had, by its massive intervention in Korea, established its full military presence in Manchuria, Russia relinquished all these rights. It can now be seen that here lay some of the seeds of the later Sino-Russian dispute.

The first task of the Communist regime, undertaken in the period from 1949 to 1955, was the rehabilitation of the country after the devastation caused by wars. At this time the base for China's industrial revolution was laid by the building of heavy industrial plants, railways, and roads, and by the modernization of cities. Order was restored throughout the country, currency was stabilized, and foreign trade began to recover. This was a period of welfare-state socialism and of industrialization rather than of real Communism. Much of what was done then should have been done many years earlier by any competent government.

At first land reform was carried out with the simple division of land among all who cultivated it; the landlord received his small share along with everyone else. The next step was the promotion of co-operative farming and of the commune system. These changes eliminated individual holdings; the former landowner received a share in the commune or in the co-operative farm's total assets. He, like everyone else, was entitled to food, housing, and education, and to a salary that was calculated on the number of work points earned. The calculation of work points took into account both the number of hours worked and the nature of the work done.

There is much dispute over whether these changes have solved the problem of Chinese peasant poverty. What is certain is that they

SOVFOTO

The Soviet Union formally recognized the new People's Republic of China on October 2, 1949—one day after Mao's regime was established. Diplomatic relations between the two countries were cordial in the 1950's—as this Russian painting of a meeting between Mao Tse-tung and Stalin suggests; but they have since become very hostile.

have fundamentally changed the nature of the problem. It is no longer a question of how many people can make a living from each tiny plot or how many will starve if the rain is scanty or excessive. All cultivators now work for communes, and the existence of communes has made it possible to organize large-scale flood control, irrigation, and crop production. The new system prevented wholesale famine when the great drought of 1960–1962 afflicted much of China. A question remains, however, as to whether in the years to come China's population will outgrow the food supply. Chinese agricultural specialists believe that if the land can be treated with chemical fertilizer in the same way as it is in Japan, the problem will not arise, even though a great increase in population is expected by the end of the century.

In 1957 the Chinese government appeared

to relax its control over publication and criticism; to artists and writers Mao Tse-tung said, "let a hundred flowers bloom." He invited scientists to let a hundred schools of thought contend. He was taken at his word by many, and a considerable volume of criticism was published in the Chinese press. Some related to matters of administration and daily life, and some was ideological and in certain instances appeared to challenge the basic positions of the Communist system. After disorders had occurred in one or two cities, the government clamped down on criticism. Some critics, who were considered to have gone too far and to have abused their new freedom by attacking the principles rather than the practices of the regime, were sent to country districts to "learn from the peasants." There was no sanguinary purge, and some of the criticisms were heeded. The Hundred Flowers movement was the first indication of a persistent element in Mao Tse-tung's thinking: his dislike of bureaucratic formality and of the bureaucratic hierarchy. The attempt to get the intellectuals to reform the party in the Hundred Flowers movement proved too unpredictable; ten years later, in the Cultural Revolution, Mao tried again, with far greater effect.

At this writing it is too soon to analyze definitively the genesis of the Great Proletarian Cultural Revolution—to give it its full name—for much is still unknown. It is believed that disagreements in the higher leadership first appeared over the policy of the Great Leap Forward, a crash program of industrialization undertaken in 1958. It is now well known that this program was not a complete success, although it was not such a failure as many critics have claimed. Disagreements among the regime's leaders became involved with the developing quarrel with Russia, a quarrel that in 1960 led to Russia's withdrawal of technical aid to China. This withdrawal was, temporarily, a hard blow, but it has not proved a lasting handicap, for it forced China to help itself and develop products and skills hitherto obtained from Russia.

The party's disagreements were probably based on differing assessments of the priorities for the revolution and the party. It seems probable that Liu Shao-ch'i, the head of state and chief organizer of the party hierarchy, believed that China's first need was the steady development of industry and agriculture, and not revolutionary commitments of a far-reaching character at home and abroad. Liu and his followers did not want to disturb the new generation, which had profited from free education and now sought to advance itself in new careers. No doubt Liu and his followers also wanted to maintain their hold on the Communist party hierarchy, and thus on the country.

Mao Tse-tung has deliberately put an end to this policy. Liu and his followers were denounced as "taking the revisionist highroad," even though they criticized the Soviet Union as fervently as Mao Tse-tung's adherents did. He raised up the Red Guards to attack not only old "bourgeois" intellectuals but the party hierarchy itself. The Red Guards have disrupted the party and driven its leaders from power. Dedicated service to the people rather than the pursuit of an individual career, which might also be of service to the nation, is now held up as the ideal for youth. No one, it is said, has the right to expect to be a leader merely because he has skill. The Red Guards dislodged the holders of power; soon, however, factional struggles broke out in their own ranks. The army has had to be called in to restore order and to help administer the provinces. It cannot be said that the situation is resolved. It is clear, however, that the original purpose of the Great Cultural Revolution has not yet been achieved. It is also evident

that the struggle is taking place within the Communist movement itself, and not between Communists and anti-Communists, despite the statements to the contrary that are being made for polemical purposes within China.

Whether the Cultural Revolution is the closing phase of the Chinese revolution that began in 1911 is still unknown. It is evident, however, that the successive phases of the revolution as a whole have greatly altered the character of the Chinese culture. The revolution, in sum, represents a great social transformation that is still continuing. It is not a movement of collapse, but rather one of dynamic change—a movement that will in one way or other generate a new and vigorous society. China will be much more dedicated to science and technology than it has been in the past and much less involved with the cultivation of the arts and humanities. The new China, born of a sweeping revolution, will never be able to return to the splendid isolation that was for so many centuries both the burden and the glory of the ancient empire.

A contemporary Swedish cartoon portrays Mao Tse-tung as a dragon; his body is composed of thousands of Chinese, who are shown chanting his praises.

KARLSSON
IN *Aftonbladet*
SWEDEN

The East is Red

In the years since the Communist party's triumph over Chiang Kai-shek's Kuomintang forces, China has undergone what Mao Tse-tung calls the Great Proletarian Cultural Revolution. The phrase is high-flown but accurate, for Chairman Mao's programs have indeed been revolutionary, and they have profoundly affected the cultural patterns of the proletariat. As part of a broad effort to realign peasant culture, which had traditionally been based on family loyalty, a massive program of resettlement was undertaken in 1958. It called for the relocation of all agricultural workers—about ninety per cent of China's population—on huge communes, patterned on Russian collective farms, but differing from the Russian models in that men were housed separately, away from their families. This audacious program met with subtle but effective resistance among the peasants, who sabotaged equipment and organized work slowdowns, which eventually forced the plan's modification. Still, much was accomplished, although not as much as the extravagant production reports and exaggerated agricultural statistics claim. By 1958 ninety-nine per cent of China's agricultural and industrial output was under state control, and food production was nearly triple that of 1946. As a result of the Cultural Revolution, China's ancient traditions were abandoned and scoffed at. "There is no Jade Emperor in Heaven," sang performers on the state radio, "There is no Dragon King on Earth." Their place seemed to have been taken by Mao Tse-tung, who has been the recipient of adulation that is almost without parallel in human history. "From Peking's golden hill," go the words of another frequently performed song, "shines forth light far and wide. Chairman Mao is the bright golden sun. Oh how warm, oh how kind, lighting up our serfs' hearts. We are marching on the broad and happy socialist road."

Youths wave banners at a celebration during Nikita Khrushchev's visit to Peking—before Russia and China quarreled. Models of missiles are at rear.

OVERLEAF: *A fireworks display in honor of the Communist revolution attracts a throng to the square in front of the People's Congress Hall in Peking.*

THE RED GUARDS

The evolution of the Red Guards from a militant student group into a Maoist terrorist band during the last months of 1966 is a striking manifestation of Mao Tse-tung's continuing ability to reassert power over the course and the character of the Great Proletarian Cultural Revolution. As instruments of Chairman Mao's will, the Red Guards proved relatively ineffective, alienating more loyal members of the Communist party and purging fewer "party enemies" than Mao probably intended. The objects of Red Guard vilification, however, were those that Mao himself has customarily railed against: bourgeois culture, revisionism, and the linked concepts of filial piety and ancestor worship—all of which undercut devotion to the state. The violence of the Red Guards' attacks on their chosen enemies is based upon the belief that there must be conflict before the new society can arrive at a valid and genuinely revolutionary solution to its problem.

"We erase the past life," proclaims the Red Guard slogan (near left) pasted over the face of a Buddha in a Hang-chou temple—and they have done precisely that. Adherents of the "past life" as well as the symbols of it have come under attack: at far left, officials are berated on huge posters for "anti-Mao behavior"; above, a Pekinese official is forced to parade in a dunce's cap that proclaims him a "political pickpocket."

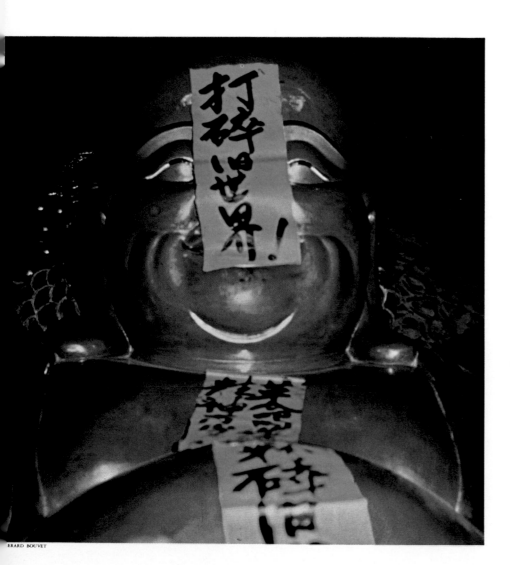

MARC RIBOUD, *Magnum*

FOOD FOR
THE MILLIONS

The advent of Communism has probably affected the peasantry more than any other segment of contemporary Chinese society. Farm life has been completely revolutionized. One aim of the upheaval was to increase productivity. Productivity has indeed increased tremendously, but it has barely kept pace with China's needs. In 1960, two years after the inauguration of the communal farming system, there was, according to one report, slightly less food available per capita than there had been in 1937. The effects of Mao's massive relocation projects, coupled with a series of formidable natural disasters, have caused harvest yields to fall consistently short of government expectations, great though those yields are. Harvests will have to continue to increase enormously in order to feed China's growing population. In the early 1960's the population grew at a rate of almost twenty millions a year, and it will reach a figure of two billions by the year 2001.

Relatively sophisticated tools, such as the rice transplanter shown at left, are becoming increasingly common on communal farms. The posed farm workers at right are studying Mao Tse-tung's writings amid hand-stacked hayricks.

Vast construction projects, such as the San-men dam (above), built rapidly and almost entirely by hand, are the pride of modern China.

THE GREAT
LEAP FORWARD

China's industrial development since 1958, the year of the Great Leap Forward, has been staggering and unprecedented. The country's total steel production, which in 1958 was identical with India's output, is now more than double that of India. Steel supplies would have been even greater if the thousands of "backyard furnaces," which were built to augment annual production, had yielded usable ore. Drawing upon its major industrial asset—almost unlimited manpower—China has created refineries, hydroelectric plants, and enormous housing developments. Construction methods are generally primitive, and errors in design have been frequent, particularly since 1960, when worsening Sino-Soviet relations prompted Moscow to withdraw some 1,300 architects, engineers, and technicians from China's industrial centers. Without help from the Russians, the Chinese were left without the special skills and, in some cases, the blueprints necessary to complete many planned projects.

Workmen labor at a hearth in a coke factory near Peking.

1. Bullets zip past the pilothouse as, with great composure, leader Chen Ta-ying issues orders to change the course. Second mate Lin Jung steers while the captain, Huang Pu-san, quickly calls for more speed.

2. The cargo hold is hit and bursts into flames. First mate Hsieh Jui-yu and seaman Hsu Chun-jui are wounded. Boatswain Huang Ta-yao jumps into the smoking hold and flails at the fire with a wet towel.

5. The boat lists sharply, but the red hearts of its crew are undaunted. As Chen Yung-shang—political commissar—gives the order to abandon ship, they gather on deck and pledge to march on to new battles.

6. The commissar is the last to leave. Standing on the slanting deck, he grimly records the U.S. imperialists' blood-debt to the Chinese people and writes a poem of China's sons' fight to the finish against the enemy.

9. Hsiung and Liang, together with the lightly injured, gather wild fruit and find fresh water in the dense forest. They themselves abstain so that the seriously wounded and older comrades can have more.

10. Liang reaches a big island and makes contact with the Vietnamese people. Their army organizes a rescue party, which helps the heroic seamen leave the uninhabited island, despite strafing by enemy planes.

ALL: *China Pictorial*, NO. 6, 1967

3. *Hearing the roar of diving enemy planes, Li Ta-tsai shields his comrade-in-arms with his body. In doing so, he writes a song of Communism with his life. Enemy planes continue to strafe the boat.*

4. *The boat is sinking, but the crew is calm and united. As they help each other into life jackets, radioman Huang Wei-chao dashes on deck, holding high the treasured book,* Quotations from Chairman Mao.

7. *Recovering consciousness, Huang pleads: "Never mind me, you are wounded too!" Hsiung and Hsu reply, "We are Communists. We'll never leave our class brother. . . . If we can pull through, so will you!"*

8. *At last the heroes reach a barren island. Bearing in mind Chairman Mao's teaching that the party is the force that leads the cause forward, Huang organizes his men in order to persist in the struggle.*

ARMED WITH
THE THOUGHT OF MAO

Mao Tse-tung has made billboards and books, newspapers and nursery rhymes—and even the venerable Peking Opera—instruments of his propaganda barrage. Party blandishments are posted on the walls of public buildings, factories, and schoolhouses, broadcast on the radio, and repeated endlessly in numerous government-published periodicals. All mediums of communication urge the Chinese to act selflessly, work diligently, and "bear in mind Chairman Mao's teachings. . . ." The cartoon strip that appears on these pages typifies Maoist propaganda. Its romanticized narrative, translated almost verbatim in the captions beneath the pictures, describes a battle that supposedly occurred in 1966. In the battle Chinese sailors, armed with the thoughts of Mao, are able to survive an American attack.

OVERLEAF: *Eighty per cent of the Chinese people were illiterate in 1951. Almost 120 million children and 130 million peasants now attend classes, which teach "social ethics" as well as reading and writing.*

PAOLA KOCH, BLACK STAR

11. *About to leave in triumph for home, the heroes thank the Vietnamese people and the party leaders. Their hosts declare: "The militant friendship between the Chinese people and ours knows no limit."*

This clay tomb figure of a horseman dates from the Wei dynasty.

Acknowledgments and Index

ACKNOWLEDGMENTS

The editors wish to express their gratitude for the valuable editorial assistance of Professor L. Carrington Goodrich, Columbia University; of Thomas Lawton, Curator of Chinese Art at the Freer Gallery of Art, Smithsonian Institution; of Professor Wen C. Fong, Princeton University; and of Wango H. C. Weng, Scarsdale, New York.

The editors also wish to acknowledge the following individuals and institutions for their generous assistance and for their co-operation in making available pictorial material in their collections:

Mr. and Mrs. James W. Alsdorf, Winnetka, Illinois
American Museum of Natural History
Art Institute of Chicago
    Jack V. Sewell
The Asia Society
    Gordon B. Washburn
James Cahill, Berkeley, California
Nigel Cameron, Hong Kong
Cincinnati Art Museum
    Carolyn Schine
City Art Museum, St. Louis
The Cleveland Museum of Art
    Jeanne Cassill
    Sherman E. Lee
Robert Crandall Associates
Danish National Museum
M. H. de Young Memorial Museum, Avery Brundage Collection
    René-Yvou Lefebvre d'Argencé
The Denver Art Museum
    Mary C. Lanius
Fine Arts Gallery, San Diego
Fogg Art Museum
    Eliza M. Webster
Marilyn Fu, Princeton, New Jersey
The Hoover Institution, Stanford University
    John T. Ma
Honolulu Academy of Arts
    Leslie B. Nerio
Richard Hsio, Princeton, New Jersey

Lois Katz, The Brooklyn Museum
Mr. and Mrs. L. Locsin, Manila, Philippines
Lucy Lo, Princeton, New Jersey
Metropolitan Museum of Art
    Fong Chow
    Marise Johnson
    Jean Schmidt
The Minneapolis Institute of Arts
Arthur Miyazawa, Tokyo
Musée Cernuschi, Paris
    Maria Therese Bobot
    Vadime Elisseeff
Musée Guimet, Paris
    Jeanine Auboyer
    Michele Parazzoli
Museum of Far Eastern Antiquities, Stockholm
Museum of Fine Arts, Boston
    Jan Fontein
Dr. Hugo Munsterberg
National Gallery of Canada
    Dr. R. H. Hubbard
National Palace Museum, Taipei, Taiwan, Republic of China
    Dr. Chiang Fu-tsung
Otto G. Nelson
William Rockhill Nelson Gallery of Art, Kansas City, Missouri
    Jeanne Harris
    Laurence Sickman
New York Public Library, Prints Division
    Elizabeth Roth
Office du Livre Fribourg
    Suzanne Meister
Peabody Museum, Salem, Massachusetts
Mr. and Mrs. Peter Quennell, London
Royal Ontario Museum, Toronto

Shio-yen Shih
Barbara Stephen
Peter Swann
Dr. Arthur M. Sackler, New York
Mr. and Mrs. Ezekiel Schloss, New York
Raymond Schwartz, Washington, D.C.
Seattle Art Museum
Dr. Paul Singer, Summit, New Jersey
Bianca Spantigati, Rome
Max Steinbook, New York
Michael Sullivan, Palo Alto, California
Mrs. David Sutherland, London
Charles E. Tuttle and Co., Inc., Tokyo
    Florence Sakade
Collection van Heydt, Rietberg Museum, Zurich
The Henry Francis du Pont Winterthur Museum, Winterthur, Delaware
Worcester Art Museum

Maps by Cal Sacks.

TRANSLITERATION

The editors have transliterated Chinese names according to the Wade-Giles system, with the exception of certain common words, such as Confucius and Shanghai, for which an accepted English version exists. In the anthology selections, however, the book departs from this practice and Chinese names are reproduced as the original translator spelled them.

194 "The Creation," "The Birth of Confucius," from *Sources of Chinese Tradition*, edited by Wm. Theodore de Bary. Copyright © 1960 Columbia University Press,

INDEX

NOTE: *Page numbers in boldface type indicate that the subject is illustrated.*

407

410